On Your Own Again

On Your Own Again

THE DOWN-TO-EARTH
GUIDE TO GETTING THROUGH
A DIVORCE OR SEPARATION
AND GETTING ON
WITH YOUR LIFE

Keith Anderson, M.D.
Roy MacSkimming

St. Martin's Press   New York

The authors wish to acknowledge Robert Wool of New York, whose early faith and encouragement got this project off the ground.

Design by Judith Christensen

Library of Congress Cataloging-in-Publication Data

Anderson, Keith.
    On your own again : the down-to-earth guide to getting through
a divorce or separation and getting on with your life / Keith Anderson
and Roy MacSkimming.
        p.   cm.
    ISBN 0-312-07757-2
    1. Divorce—United States.   2. Divorced people—United States—
-Psychology.   I. MacSkimming, Roy.   II. Title.
HQ834.A693   1992
 306.89—dc20   92-4956
                                                                   CIP

First Edition: October 1992

10 9 8 7 6 5 4 3 2 1

This book is dedicated to Sarah and Mark:
"We know—it happened to us."

Contents

To the Reader

In our first session together, I always ask new patients one simple question: Why are you here?

They've gone to a certain amount of trouble to see me, I remind them—to obtain a referral, to make an appointment, to wait several weeks and then show up in my office at the appointed hour. Why are they doing this? What do they want?

The answers I receive are many and varied: "My best friend sent me." "I'm impossible to live with." "My husband left me and I can't cope." "I'm here to save my marriage."

These answers are honest enough, but they don't reveal the deeper reason why most men and women in pain come to see me—or any other therapist. Or why they pick up a book such as this one.

Naturally, people are looking for relief from the pain and confusion they're suffering. But there's an even more fundamental motive for seeking professional help: a profound need to learn how to *be* in the world—how to know, and become, your own unique self.

In therapy, the patient makes a commitment to work on behalf of him- or herself. Similarly with you, the reader of this book. You're someone who knows about pain and confusion. You don't need to be told that the only thing worse than separation is a bad relationship. But you're determined that pain and confusion aren't going to be your permanent lot in life.

My focus, therefore, isn't on saving or losing a marriage or relationship, as important as that may be, or may have been in the past. There is something even more important: the vital and enduring issue of learning to be yourself—in or out of a relationship.

That's what *On Your Own Again* is really all about. By opening this book and starting to read, you've made a statement about yourself. You're asking the crucial question that will let you deal with the rest of your life. You're saying, "My relationship is coming (or has come) apart; I'm desperately unhappy; my partner is unhappy; the kids (if any) are unhappy; everybody's unhappy." And you're asking, "What am I going to do about it?"

The significance of posing this question is that you're preparing for change. You're signaling your readiness to take steps on your own behalf, to begin anew, and thus to embark on a process of change that will lead you, after many twists and turns, toward personal growth and happiness.

Amazingly enough, the goals of personal growth and happiness can be achieved whether your relationship continues or not. This is often difficult to realize. You've lived so much of your adult life as one half of a couple that your personal identity seems swallowed up—seemingly merged with your partner's identity or with the identity of the marriage itself—and as a result, you wonder how much of *you* survives.

Later on, we'll look at reasons why this merging of identities takes place. And we'll look at the ways you can be yourself once again, whether in or out of a relationship. For the moment, consider, if you will, a radical notion: When you're making the necessary changes in your life, *your partner is irrelevant*. You're doing it for *yourself*. Because no matter what happens to your marital status, you've got to be yourself—a person in your own right.

In the broadest sense, then, the answer to "What am I going to do about it?" is: "I'm going to be me."

On Your Own Again is divided into four parts. This structure corresponds to the four psychological stages of surviving separation and divorce. While it's true that every life is unique, and everyone's suffering special, there does exist a typical and predictable pattern in the long process of renewal after separation. In my professional experience, the great majority of men and women pass through these four developmental stages.

Even more remarkable, the four stages typically follow a sequence that stretches over approximately three years. It can be extremely helpful to know that your personal path to recovery and renewal is marked by guideposts along the way.

These stages aren't as clear-cut and identifiable as the more familiar milestones of separation, such as your first meeting with the lawyer, the day you sign the separation agreement, the final decree from the court, the first Thanksgiving or Christmas or anniversary after the breakup. Such "marker" events can evoke strong emotions, bringing back feelings of distress or sadness over the breakup.

No, the stages I'm talking about vary in length for different people, and may even overlap to some extent. They aren't so distinct that you can say, "I'm finishing Stage One today and starting Stage Two tomorrow." Each individual passes through them at his or her own pace. But roughly speaking, the stages evolve one out of the other, according to the following pattern:

Stage One: *Hurting*—the first three months or so.
Stage Two: *Exploring*—the balance of Year One.
Stage Three: *Becoming You*—Year Two.
Stage Four: *Getting Comfortable*—Year Three.

Don't worry if your experience doesn't fit closely with this timetable. Different individuals will move through these stages at their own rates. But the stages give you a framework to hang your experience on—and to help you know you're moving in the right direction as you learn to live successfully, on your own again.

Incidentally, I never advise people to divorce. It's such a life-shaping decision that every individual must make it for him- or herself. But by the same token, I never tell people to marry, either.

If you're contemplating separation, this book won't tell you which way to jump. It will, however, explore the urgent problems that newly separated or newly divorced people must typically deal with. And by clarifying those problems, it will help you to see what's at stake, enabling you to make up your mind about your own relationship.

If, on the other hand, you're already separated or divorced, this book will serve as a survival guide through unfamiliar and seemingly hostile territory. It will help you to understand and work through the pain you're feeling. And it will put you, I hope, on familiar and even comfortable terms with the often unpredictable, sometimes baffling, but potentially deeply rewarding experience of being on your own again.

Stage One
Hurting

The first hundred days are the toughest.

It's painful enough to live through the sad and angry times leading up to your separation. But during the first three months of being on your own, you're confronted by the sheer awesomeness of this new stage in your life. Much of the time you feel shaken. Sometimes you feel overwhelmed by uncertainty and fear. The first three chapters of this book are designed to help get you through this difficult stage and on to the next.

For now, your priority is just surviving from day to day. We'll be examining different ways to manage that. And we'll look at the parallels between a separation and a death—both of which involve a need to grieve—always keeping in mind that it's a relationship, not a human being, that has died. Finally, we'll consider some of the typical pitfalls newly separated people encounter, and how to deal with them.

Reading these chapters may hurt a little, may touch on some raw spots in your feelings. But then, so much in your life hurts right now. Is this stage just as bad for everyone else? Absolutely. The main thing to remember is that it does come to an end.

Chapter One

Coming Apart

"All happy families are alike, but each unhappy family is unhappy in its own way."

Leo Tolstoy, *Anna Karenina*

"It's a terrifying thing to split up."

Danny DeVito, after directing his black
comedy about divorce, *The War of the Roses*

Danny DeVito may be no Tolstoy, but he hit it dead-on: When a marriage or other primary relationship comes apart, we get scared. And panicky. And angry. Although we may not act out these emotions with all the hysteria, obsessiveness, and vengeful violence of Mr. and Mrs. Rose in DeVito's movie, *The War of the Roses*, the emotions are there all the same—powerful and overwhelming. They goad us into acting in disturbing and unexpected ways. Sometimes they just tear us apart inside. Very few experiences, outside of actual armed combat, can push us so far over the edge into downright fear and loathing.

Few experiences can rival the trauma of a couple in the throes of splitting up—when the relationship is outwardly intact, but in a state of meltdown within. Practically nothing compares with the crushing sadness, the heartbreaking disappointment, the bitter disillusionment, the raging anger. The pain of it all.

This tends to be true no matter what the relationship was like in earlier days: whether it was once good or bad, brief or long, serene or stormy, adulterous or monogamous. And regardless of whether we resist the breakup or encourage it to happen, it usually turns out to feel even worse than we anticipated. As the relationship comes apart, the sense of imminent loss is enormous. The prospect of facing an unknown, unexpected future as a single person can be terrifying indeed.

This reaction is pretty well universal—in other words, normal. Yet it comes to each of us in different forms. As Tolstoy pointed out in *Anna Karenina,* each unhappy family is unhappy in its own way. He was talking about unhappy relationships, too.

One patient told me about going with her husband on a long-planned beach vacation to South Carolina just before they separated. She felt desolate, she said, as the two of them sat together in grim silence on the sand. The spectacle of other couples enjoying themselves nearby made her realize that her own once-vibrant marriage was truly finished, and nothing would ever be the same.

Another patient described walking past the hospital where he'd witnessed the birth of his two children several years earlier. The mere sight of that red-brick building made him break down in tears at the thought that he and his wife would never again experience such a time of hope and joy.

While going through the breakup of her marriage, a social worker—an intelligent, attractive woman, highly skilled at helping emotionally disturbed people—told me of her crippling sense of helplessness and panic at the idea of starting over as a single person. She could counsel others effectively, but not herself.

These are just three of the many faces of separation. All three of these individuals not only survived the experience, but are now leading rewarding new lives. Yet during the period when their marriages were coming apart, they all suffered through their own special agony.

When you think about it, the agony is inevitable. A life-structure that once appeared solid, safe, and secure is crumbling. A relationship that once formed the bedrock of your existence has turned out to contain a crack as profound as the San Andreas Fault. A commitment once based on mutual love and respect is dying—being replaced by conflict, anger, even abuse—and you feel helpless to save it. No wonder this is a terrible time.

From personal experience, I know how terrible it can be. In addition to counseling many men and women in the aftermath of separation and divorce, I've gone through the process myself. But I've also seen how frequently the end of a relationship, however agonizing, can ultimately prove to be highly beneficial for both parties: a necessary step toward building better lives.

A PREDICTABLE PATTERN

Because of where you are in your life right now, it may seem hard to believe, but the disorientation, disillusionment, and pain of splitting up won't last forever.

When I treat men and women who have recently separated from their partners, experience tells me they'll progress through a predictable cycle of psychological growth. The cycle contains four developmental stages, each one growing out of the last. There is a pattern—a pattern of lows and highs—leading to recovery and renewal after separation and divorce. This doesn't mean I have any miracles to offer, or any pain-free cures for getting over a shattered relationship. But there is reassurance in knowing a pattern does exist, a path leading to higher ground.

What's more, for most people the four stages follow an approximate timetable, as described in the section at the beginning, "To the Reader." But for now, we'll concentrate on what happens when a marriage—or any other long-standing love relationship—comes apart. And how to tell if there's any hope it could be put back together again.

TO SPLIT OR NOT TO SPLIT

When your primary relationship is troubled, you feel despair. Things between you and your partner have gone terribly wrong. Try as you might, you scarcely know where to turn or how to make it all right again. You're torn by conflicting emotions: love and hate, rage and guilt, hope and despair. They drag you first one way, then the other. Impulses toward forgiveness and compromise are succeeded by the conviction that your partner has gone too far this time—that he or she has said or done the unforgivable, and it's all over.

Such deep and abiding discord seems beyond remedy. Instead of clearing the air, fighting just seems to dig the two of you deeper into a hole of mutual hostility and ill will. You're desperate to get your bearings, to find some direction or some solution; it's as if someone has shot out all the lights, leaving you in total darkness.

At such a dark and anxious time, you suffer a devastating sense of loss. It feels like a death—of love, of your romantic ideals, of your hopes for a solid family life with its lifelong emotional security. You don't know who's to blame—you, your partner, both of you at once—or whether it's right to blame anyone at all.

And yet, you still haven't decided to separate once and for all. No matter how tense or awful life is at home, no matter how dissatisfied you are with your relationship, the idea of leaving is even more horrendous. That's the big step, the truly traumatic one: crossing the Rubicon into the land of the single.

One moment, you're tantalized by fantasies of how wonderfully liberating and fulfilling it will be to live on your own again; the next moment, you're scared silly by nightmare imaginings of how lonely it will feel. Which version of your future is true? Perhaps neither. Perhaps both.

Should you make an all-out, last-ditch effort to rededicate yourself to saving the relationship? Or should you resign yourself to the fact that you can't get blood out of a stone? As with so much else right now, you just can't be sure.

At this stage, people fall into one of two broad categories: those with options and those without options.

PEOPLE WITHOUT OPTIONS

Men and women who still enjoy options have to decide whether to end or to continue a troubled relationship: whether to leave, kick the bum out, or arrive at a mutual decision with their partner to try again. Those are tough choices to have to make. But people without options are in an even tougher spot. Their partners have presented them with a *fait accompli*, leaving them no choices. They've been left, dumped for someone else, or kicked out of the house, and there isn't much they can do about it.

If there's a silver lining for these people, it's that they now know where they stand. At least they can get on with their lives. But if you ask them at the time, they'll never say they feel fortunate. Needless to say, it's impossible to feel good about having separation thrust upon you.

For example, your husband arrives home from a long business

trip. Despite recent difficulties in the marriage, you're ready to show him how much you've missed him. Then he announces, "I've met this woman I'm crazy about. It's love. I've decided to pack my bags and move in with her. Don't try to talk me out of it."

Or you come home with a bouquet of roses in your hand, determined to kiss your wife and make up, and then some, only to find that she and the kids and the furniture are gone, and a "For Sale" sign stands on the front lawn. She just couldn't stand any more wrangling, so she pulled a *coup de grace*. (Don't scoff—this happens more often than you might think!)

For others, a court order lends a brutal finality to a relationship. I once knew a husband who was evicted from his house and marriage, but not for the reasons you might assume. Bernie wasn't a drunk or a wife-abuser or even a philanderer, just the most passive man I've ever known—a guy who hated getting involved, emotionally or socially. Bernie constantly busied himself with his lawn and hedges, or chores in his basement workshop, so he wouldn't have to talk to his wife or kids or neighbors. His wife—a decent, likable woman—spent years trying to communicate with him, to make improvements in their life together. She pleaded with him to go for marital counseling, but he flatly refused. "What's the problem? Nothing's wrong," he'd always insist.

Finally, she told Bernie she wanted a separation—but he wouldn't even consider it. At her wits' end, and faced with the endless prospect of living with an emotional cipher, she sought legal advice about her rights. Eventually, she was able to obtain a court order requiring Bernie to leave the marital home. As his last act, he finally displayed some feeling: In revenge, he went next door to cut his neighbor's lawn instead of his own.

An even more troubling situation where there is no choice is in the event of physical abuse in the home. If a spouse (usually the wife) or child is being physically or sexually abused, it's absolutely mandatory to leave, even if temporarily. No ifs or buts about it: In our society, nobody has the right to assault another human being. Being married does not confer that right. Nor does being a partner, parent, or provider.

Since leaving the home usually involves risk and sacrifice, it can be extremely difficult for a person to decide to get out of an abusive relationship. Some women stay out of fear of retribution: "He'll come and get me, and then things will *really* be bad." Some stay out of fear of poverty or of the unknown: "Oh well, he just hits me from time to time, when he's had too much to drink, and then he feels sorry about it afterwards. Mostly he's pretty decent. And we have a nice home and . . . how would I ever manage on my own anyway? How would the kids and I survive?"

But the real question is, How will the kids and you survive in the event of continued abuse? Assault is a criminal act, and for good reason. If you or the children have been attacked, or if you have cause to fear retribution, the police are there to protect you—that's their job. You also have relatives, friends, or neighbors you can turn to for shelter, food, financial help, and, above all, emotional support.

Most communities have resources of one kind or another to help you deal with such an emergency: a crisis telephone line for abuse victims, a shelter for battered women or homeless families, a children's aid society. Through social workers, legal-aid organizations, or a lawyer, you can obtain advice about your legal rights and remedies. If necessary, your lawyer can seek a restraining order from the court to keep an abusive partner away from you and the children.

Help and protection do exist for abused partners and families. (And increasingly, counseling and group therapy are available for abusers as well.) If you have been abused, you have to seek that help and protection. Often that means you have to leave the abusive situation and possibly the relationship, too.

In some cases the problem eventually can be resolved, and you can go back. But for now, your physical safety is the most important thing. Leaving may seem like a terrible step, but you've got to take it.

PEOPLE WITH OPTIONS

Men and women with options, on the other hand, may be found in a great variety of situations. Some may feel profoundly alienated from their partner or permanently unfulfilled; others may just be bored and restless. Some are involved with another person; others are wounded by a partner's infidelity. Some have to choose between a career move and a spouse's desire for stability; others find that they and their partners have failed to grow or have grown in different directions over the years, to the point where they no longer share the same interests, goals, or values.

Any number of combinations of these and other factors is possible. What all such situations have in common, however, is that the relationship can be termed ill. The key question is whether the illness is terminal.

People often go into therapy seeking an answer to that question. Patients come to see me in the hope that I can offer an instant cure for an ailing relationship or a final judgment on a marriage's life expectancy—a confirmation that it's either worth saving or beyond hope. In reality, I have no such Solomonic wisdom to offer.

I always explain that it's up to the individual to arrive at his or her own judgment, to answer the question in the way that feels right. Some relationships *are* terminally ill, whereas others have only recently entered a critical condition—as a result of some especially bitter dispute, say, or the revelation of an affair. The person living inside the relationship knows best if enough vital life-signs remain to make it worth trying again, despite whatever grievances he or she may have. All I can do is help patients to reexamine their relationship thoroughly and honestly.

If your husband comes home and says, as the one above did, "I've fallen in love with Mary and I'm moving in with her," that's one thing—your marriage is probably over, and the sooner you face up to it and start acting in your own best interests, the better. But if he comes home and says, "I've fallen in love with Mary and I don't know what to do—please forgive me," that could mean another thing altogether. Then you may have a lot of work ahead of you.

In Chapter 4, "Meeting Your Adult Needs," we'll consider the psychological dynamics of marriage that lead grown-up men and women to make mommies or daddies out of their spouses. That chapter clarifies why a husband would ask his wife for permission to be in love with someone else while remaining married. For now, suffice it to say that this couple could probably use some counseling—individually, together, or both. Counseling could help them look at where they're going in their lives and to decide what they really want.

When the woman whose husband seeks permission for his affair finds herself responding with maternal understanding and indulgence, her behavior likely reflects the pattern of their relationship. Obviously, that pattern isn't serving her well. What she really needs is to sort out her own priorities in life. If one of those priorities is achieving a better relationship with her husband, despite his infidelity, then she should seek his agreement to visit a competent marital therapist together. Jointly, they can explore the possibility of reconciling their differences and try to rebuild their relationship on a stronger basis of mutual trust and shared values.

In counseling, there are three basic things to be considered: your life, your partner's life, and the relationship. They aren't all the same thing. Some issues are shared in common—such as the importance both of you place on fidelity to each other. But other issues are unique to the individual—issues affecting your own personal needs for growth and happiness—and have to be worked out for yourself.

Hence, you may want to consider both individual and joint therapy. Some therapists will see people only on an individual basis. Others will provide conjoint or marital therapy—will "do couples," as we say. Whatever type of therapist you choose—a psychiatrist, psychologist, social worker, or religious or community counselor—just make sure that he or she is qualified to practice (i.e., is registered with the appropriate professional governing body) in your jurisdiction. You can obtain a referral for therapy from your family doctor, lawyer, religious adviser, or friend.

In individual therapy, I should emphasize, your partner is, in a real sense, irrelevant. There, the central question for each man or woman is the same: What are *my* individual needs? And what am I doing to meet them, whether inside or outside the relationship?

Let's look at three troubled relationships, similar in some ways yet different in others, where counseling led to three distinct outcomes.

SHEILA: LEAVING UNILATERALLY

In some relationships, it's possible for the individuals involved to discuss their problems constructively and to decide collaboratively, "This isn't working out. We're going to separate." In other relationships, such collaboration just isn't possible.

The latter was the case with a patient I'll call Sheila: a thirty-nine-year-old insurance agent with two children, aged fifteen and thirteen. Sheila's husband, Norm, wanted to run her life. In the early years of their marriage, when the kids were small, she'd pretty much let him—she'd been too busy and preoccupied to fight Norm's controlling behavior and instead had concentrated on making a good home life for the family.

But when the children were older and needed her less, Sheila decided to return to the work force. It was a turning point in the marriage. Sheila had to put up a tremendous, determined struggle to overcome Norm's opposition. He wanted her to stay home and cook and keep house; although he claimed this was because he and the children needed her in the home, his real concern was that Sheila would be harder to control after acquiring the independence that a job and salary would bring.

After Sheila went back to work, Norm's manipulating style, previously low-key, turned overtly nasty. His abuse wasn't physical, but verbal: constant, carping demands about domestic matters; nitpicking criticisms of meals or the state of the kitchen; or comments about the way she was letting the children "get away with murder." Kindness and tenderness were forgotten. There was no longer any emotional sharing or nurturing in the marriage, just a toxic black cloud of tension always hanging in the air. The tension was poisoning the children's lives, too, since they also became targets of their father's tyrannical bluster.

Sheila was sustained during this difficult period by two sources of emotional support: her church, where she was very active and made several warm friendships, and her weekly therapy sessions with me. Gradually, as Norm's conduct worsened, she developed greater confidence in her own strengths. At last, Sheila's resolve hardened; she decided she'd had enough, and the time had come to take action.

She saw a lawyer to ascertain her legal position. Then she found a place for herself and the children to live as an interim measure. The lawyer sent Norm a letter informing him of Sheila's intention to move out with the children, phrasing it in a way that would discourage Norm from turning violent or trying to stop her. With the assistance of her church minister, Sheila removed clothes, some household items, and necessary pieces of furniture from the house to her new apartment. Thus, she used her community resources to deal with her husband from a position of strength.

Sheila's decision to leave wasn't precipitated by any one dramatic event, but a long accumulation of blows and hurts over the years. The decision was hers and hers alone. Unfortunately, it wasn't possible to get Norm to discuss the problem rationally and arrive at a mutually acceptable solution. When she tried, he'd merely tell her to stop being silly and to give up her church work and spend more time at home, reorganizing the pots in the kitchen again because she'd certainly messed them up.

JIM: TOUGHING IT OUT

Although Jim was also in a very difficult marriage, he opted for a resolution quite different from Sheila's. But it was a choice appropriate to his psychology and to the dynamics of his relationship.

Jim, forty-three, was a free-lance magazine writer with a long history of depression. His wife, Kate, was a successful partner in a law firm. In the first decade of their marriage, Jim had been hospitalized several times when he simply could no longer cope with the combined demands of his career, his competitive, perfectionist wife, and their precocious but temperamental young son. A pattern had developed: Jim would fall apart and go into care, leaving Kate to take charge of everything at home in addition to her high-pressure job. Their relationship became firmly established on this basis: She was well, he was sick; she was the boss, he was the fruitcake.

That dynamic led to a lot of unhappy times. The marriage was really miserable, marked by frequent fights and an ongoing power struggle. Jim took plenty of criticism and verbal abuse from Kate on the grounds of his weakness, incompetence, and so forth, to which he responded by gamely fighting back when he had the strength; when he didn't, he'd fulfill Kate's predictions by collapsing and taking to bed. Then Kate would soften and look after him until he felt better, at which point the abuse and counterabuse would start all over again.

Jim often thought of leaving Kate but never felt free to go. After all, he told himself, hadn't she always tolerated his sickness in the past, taking care of him every time he'd broken down? What if he went out on his own but got sick again? Where would he find anyone who'd put up with him the way Kate had? And then there was their son—with Jim's track record, he'd never get custody.

Jim's was a classic case of someone trapped in a catch-22 marriage, with no apparent option but to hunker down and tough it out. Fortunately, however, he had an ace in the hole: his writing.

A former therapist had counseled Jim to avoid the stress of magazine deadlines because it would just precipitate a breakdown, but when Jim began seeing me, I took the opposite tack. He had a real flair for writing gossipy, bitchy, and insightful features on Hollywood stars and male-female relationships, which were published in the glossy, top-paying women's magazines. This was practically his only source of pride and self-esteem. I urged him not only to continue writing, but to do more of it, more than the odd feature two or three times a year.

"But, Doctor, what if I crack up again?" he asked fearfully.

"If that happens," I replied, "we'll deal with it. But until then, write your heart out. Think of the extra money you'll make. You won't have to depend on Kate so much. And you'll get more fun out of life."

Gradually, Jim increased his output. He greatly improved his reputation for professional reliability and even branched out into teaching a journalism course. Now he's considered—and, more important, considers himself—a success. Even Kate is impressed. She practically never has to nurse Jim back to health anymore; as a result, she's freer to concentrate on the demands and rewards of her legal career. Now she, too, is happier and denigrates Jim less. And because Jim's self-confidence has grown, his relationship with his now-teenage son has improved. The son is getting over his anger at having a dad who always fell apart when the son needed him.

JENNIFER: SITTING ON THE FENCE

Unlike Sheila, who left, or Jim, who stayed, Jennifer is still trying to keep her options open. Jennifer thinks she needs her marriage to Don for some things, but not others. She's planning to leave

Don as soon as she finishes her college degree and can afford to support herself. In the meantime, she's half in her marriage, half out.

Jennifer, thirty-two, has three children between the ages of six and eleven. She worked for three years as an executive secretary until Don, a rising young sales manager in the same company, whisked her off to the suburbs. Since then, they've traded up twice and now inhabit three thousand square feet of air-conditioned broadloom on a half-acre lot with a pool, Jacuzzi, and three cars. (Why the third car? Jennifer has never found out.)

As far as Jennifer is concerned, the main problem with Don is that he's too damned perfect—so perfect that he makes her feel stupid. He shoots below eighty at golf, water-skis circles around her, bakes a mean soufflé, and earns enough money for both of them. With only a high school diploma, Jennifer made up her mind to close the gap between them.

First, she worked as a neighborhood Mary Kay cosmetics representative to make some money of her own. She volunteered at her kids' school, helping out the coach of the swim team—a ruggedly handsome guy she developed a big crush on. Then she enrolled in a business program at the local college.

Don said, "I'll help you with your essays." Jennifer said, "You will *not*. You won't even *read* them."

She knew he'd point out all the flaws in her writing and make her feel incompetent, as usual. But she agreed to let him take her computer disks to the office and get the essays beautifully laser-printed. Don broke his promise and read the essays, coming home with piles of helpful ideas for how Jennifer could improve them.

"I could have made his changes and got an A-plus," Jennifer told me. "But then it wouldn't have been my work—I'd never have known if I could pass on my own. So I ended up with a B average, which is just fine, and I was happy. Only I was mad as hell at him."

When she went back to school, Jennifer got Don to agree to some basic changes in the division of labor around the house. He started making some of the meals, supervising the children and some of their activities, and doing some of the laundry. Don discovered there was a lot more to running the household than he'd realized. But he was still patronizing her; he did the laundry in a patronizing sort of way. His attitude was: Jennifer's going through a phase—she'll get over this, but in the meantime I'll be a saint and do the laundry.

Then she stopped having sex with him.

The fact was, Jennifer was having an affair with one of her professors at the college. Don didn't know about it, and he didn't understand why she turned away from him in bed at night, asking, "Please, don't touch me, not right now." He decided it was just part of this phase she was going through. He acted saintly about that, too, hoping things would eventually return to normal.

So far, they haven't. Jennifer is quietly planning to leave him in a couple of years, when she gets it all together—only she's not telling him. Meanwhile, Don is becoming increasingly anxious and unhappy. He's wondering, "When the hell is she going to get better?" And their relationship is growing increasingly empty—a shell, containing three thousand square feet of broadloomed, air-conditioned nothingness.

DRAWING CONCLUSIONS

Although the above three marriages have certain characteristics in common, they produced quite different results.

Sheila, Jim, and Jennifer married people who were initially "stronger"—or to be precise, dominant—in the relationship. All three struggled, with the support of therapy, to develop greater personal strength and independence through activities outside the marriage; this, in turn, had an impact on relations within the marriage. The contrasting outcomes say a lot about how these patients saw themselves and their spouses.

For Sheila, Norm's rigidity, meanness, and lack of concern for her led to the conclusion that there was no longer any real benefit to remaining in a barren relationship. Leaving was tough for Sheila, but necessary.

For Jim, it made sense to stay with Kate after learning to meet his own needs to be creative, productive, and valued as a competent adult. Even though their marriage had its flaws (to which they had both contributed), Kate proved capable of recognizing and accepting his needs and did express love for her sometimes difficult husband.

For Jennifer, the imperative to grow as a person in her own right, beyond Don's dominant presence, was healthy and natural. But sometimes she perverted this legitimate need for autonomy into a power struggle, a competition where she racked up private victories for the sake of cutting Don down to size in her mind. As a result, honesty, authenticity, and affection slowly drained out of their relationship.

BEING YOURSELF

In therapy, as in life, the question for each person is always: "What am I doing to meet my own needs—in and out of this relationship?"

For example, Don wasn't getting what he needed out of the marriage any more than Jennifer was. Instead of playing the saint and waiting for his wife to "come around," he too had to decide what he really wanted from life—to see himself as a person, with legitimate individual needs, and not merely as someone playing the role of husband and father, provider and caretaker. In Chapter 4, we'll look more closely at this business of role-playing in relationships—seeing the other person and yourself as *objects*, yoked together in mutual servitude—and why it leads to unhappiness.

What you really have to be concerned about is being yourself. Your partner is irrelevant. If you forget who *you* are and what *you* need, and instead confine yourself to playing your role, doing all the "right" things for the sake of maintaining the relationship, you fall into the trap of *not being* yourself. And if you're not being yourself—yet still clinging to your "commitment" to the relationship—then who *are* you being?

In that case, I would suggest that *you* aren't truly in the relationship at all—which makes it all rather pointless. If you think, "I have to stay in this lousy relationship because he/she needs me, the kids need me, I'm doing it all for them," you're not doing anyone a favor—not your partner, not your kids, and least of all yourself—because you're not being real; not being yourself.

Being yourself starts now. One day, Jennifer wanted to go for a bicycle ride but found a problem with the bike chain. She thought aloud that she'd take the chain to get repaired, but Don told her not to be silly, he'd fix it himself and save them money. Fuming, Jennifer gave in, but thought, "When I leave him, I'll be able to do it my way."

In reality, Jennifer could do it her way right now. She's perfectly free to go ahead and get her bike fixed at the store; she doesn't need Don's permission. Or, if she really wants to feel competent and save money too, she can attend a mini-workshop on bicycle repair or buy a how-to book on the subject. Taking one of these small but practical steps to become less dependent on Don would help Jennifer feel better and would have more constructive consequences than any number of secret acts motivated by revenge. For one thing, if she were less dependent, she would feel less angry.

For Jennifer, the real issue is to take steps *today* to feel more competent, rather than waiting until she leaves Don. He's irrelevant to her ability to change. Instead, Jennifer fantasizes about escape. As long as she imagines Don as "too damned perfect," too powerful, she'll continue feeling subservient, inadequate, angry, and compelled to run away. Finally she'll move into a new apartment, and one day she'll want to go cycling. She'll discover the bike needs repairing again—and she'll think despairingly, "If only Don were here, he'd fix it in a minute." And she'll still feel powerless.

In some relationships, one or both partners are rigid and unyielding, like Sheila's husband, Norm. But sometimes, once challenged, they can be surprisingly flexible and open to change. Don has already shown a degree of willingness to adapt to Jennifer's needs, even if he still has a lot to learn. If Jennifer can keep trying to change constructively and Don can respond likewise, she may find she doesn't have to leave him after all. Joint marital counseling could get some of the unspoken issues—such as the sexual one—onto the table, where they could be dealt with openly and honestly. If Jennifer isn't willing to make that effort, however, she ought to have the courage to make a clean break and leave Don, rather than using him. It amounts to psychological abuse to stay with a partner just because you fear being on your own.

The decision to separate is always painful and overwhelming.

But if you're making the changes necessary to meet your adult needs (which we'll get into later) and your partner refuses to accept those changes in you, then the decision to separate becomes a little easier.

If your partner responds positively, on the other hand, there may be grounds to stay in the relationship. You may decide you can still thrive as a person. And you'll begin to see your partner as a person, too—not merely as someone who makes you mad.

INTRODUCING CAROL AND BILL

In the rest of this book, I'll be addressing women and men who find themselves on their own again. I'll be talking about what their needs are and how they can be met. In the end, however, the book's ideas apply to just about any of us seeking personal growth and happiness, no matter what our situation in life.

I'll be illustrating these ideas through stories of people who've lived them out. All the names and personal details have been changed to protect individual identities. In addition, two fictionalized patients of mine—composites of real people—will appear in each chapter, living through their personal defeats and victories, their struggles to cope with separation and divorce. Let's call them Carol and Bill.

Carol and Bill will prove how capable people are of changing for the better and growing into competent, self-determining adults after the trauma of divorce. When they first came to see me, both Carol and Bill were still married—although not to each other. In fact, they've never met. But they do have certain things in common: me, for one.

CAROL

When she began treatment, Carol was thirty-seven—an intelligent, well-educated, well-groomed personnel manager for a medium-sized corporation. She'd been married to Richard, a junior executive, for fourteen years and had no children.

There was something very poignant about Carol. She was vaguely but pervasively unhappy. "I can't quite put my finger on the problem," she told me at our first session. "Part of it seems to be the way Richard and I communicate. I'm not a very open person, whereas he's probing and analytical. He's aggressive, and I have trouble saying no. So I sort of leave it to him to make the decisions. . . . I think I'm having a midlife crisis. But I feel like I'm being pushed into it."

In fact, it was Richard who had persuaded Carol to seek therapy. He thought she needed it. He always knew what was best for Carol.

Carol had grown up on the West Coast, the oldest of three daughters of a scientist father and homemaker mother. Carol was an excellent student but always felt self-conscious and inferior about being overweight. She didn't enjoy much of a social life in high school. During her university years, she lived at home, did well in her bachelor of science program, and joined a sorority, but she had no real boyfriends—until Richard.

Carol met him on a blind date during her senior year. Richard was taking a master's degree in geology—he always seemed a little bit ahead of her, in one way or another. He rescued her from social oblivion and her poor self-image. He made her feel attractive. She even lost some weight.

After graduation, they married and came East, where they both found good jobs, and Richard started molding Carol into what he wanted from a wife.

She recalled, "I felt I had to give up things, not interfere with his plans for us. Richard demanded a very exclusive relationship. But that was all right—I was grateful just to have it."

Over the years, no matter how hard Richard tried to shape Carol and teach her to come up to his standards, she never quite measured up. Her taste in clothes lacked imagination. On the tennis court, her serve and backhand were hopeless. At dinner parties, she was dull and never had anything interesting to say. The problem, Richard finally decided, lay in Carol's inability to open up and express her feelings. He had been seeing a psychiatrist and had discovered how to share emotions. Maybe if she learned the same thing, she'd become interesting after all. Richard sent her to me to get "fixed."

I soon saw that Carol's real problem was Richard. She'd discovered early in their relationship that expressing her feelings was all very well, as long as they were the feelings Richard wanted to hear. She tried to learn what he wanted, but sometimes she guessed wrong, and he reacted with irritation or anger. So she inhibited her feelings and opinions—only to be accused by Richard of being too inhibited.

When I asked Carol why she'd come to see me, she replied: "I feel like I've been on the sidelines all my life. I'm so closed up, I need to share more. I want help in trying to become a person." I really liked that last line.

Although Carol felt baffled and lost, she impressed me. She had all this potential—only she didn't realize it. Richard's ministrations hadn't helped. Carol felt that if anything went wrong in the marriage, it was all her fault. And as the marriage faltered, her self-image grew worse.

Carol imagined that if only she could learn to express her thoughts and feelings better, she and Richard would have a wonderful life together. She was terribly afraid he might leave her.

"I have to prevent that from happening," she told me. "I want to be a person so I can save my marriage."

It's great that she wants to be a person, I thought to myself. Who cares if it saves the marriage?

BILL

The forty-year-old son of hard-working immigrants, Bill took a pretty traditional view of himself and his role in the world. The oldest in a family of five children, Bill had grown up feeling responsible for helping out at home. He began working full-time at seventeen, contributing to the financial support of his family. Ten years later he started his own retail carpet business, in partnership with his two younger brothers. Before long, he bought them both out; they just didn't work hard enough to suit him.

When Bill was twenty-eight, he married Marie, who was eight years younger than he. Marie had flaming red hair, hazel-green eyes, and an Irish temper. She was the apple of her lawyer-father's eye—a touch spoiled and used to expecting a lot from life. To

Marie at twenty, Bill had seemed a good catch: a solid, reliable guy with excellent business prospects, someone who loved and indulged her and didn't mind playing Daddy-Caretaker to her Charming-Young-Thing.

But when Bill came to see me, it wasn't his idea—it was Marie's. Now thirty-two, after twelve long years of marriage, she felt a deep dissatisfaction with her life. She frequently complained that Bill worked such long hours at the store he was hardly ever home; and when he was, he'd act tired and irritable with their children, Lisa and Jordan. What's more, Marie claimed, Bill neglected her, sitting up past midnight at the dining room table going over customer invoices and accounts payable and receivable. They never had fun together, never went anywhere.

Marie resented being treated like an object. Bill just wasn't emotionally available to her, and she couldn't take it anymore. One night, she blurted out: "Oh, I don't know, Bill, I can't seem to get through to you—maybe you should go see a shrink or something. Then maybe you'd understand what the hell I'm talking about!"

Bill was mystified by Marie's reaction. Hadn't he ticked all the right boxes in life? Hadn't he been a good husband and father, a good provider? He'd bought them the beautiful new Cape Cod–style home in the right neighborhood, near the right schools. He always managed to make it for Lisa's dance recitals or Jordan's Little League games, even if he missed dinner sometimes. And he captured it all on the camcorder—those moments that proved they were one big happy, healthy, normal family. Why, just last month, he'd arranged for the photographer to come in for half a Sunday and shoot expensive color portraits of the four of them, posed smilingly with their cocker spaniel, Muffy.

Yet Marie was unhappy—boy, was she fed up! Life at home was tense.

"Can you tell me what's going on, Doctor?" Bill asked, slumped in the chair beside the fish tank in my office. "Have I done something wrong? Because if I have, just tell me and I'll fix it up."

Bill was a problem solver, a fixer, accustomed to being in charge. But he couldn't fix this problem: He couldn't even *see* it yet. He had no insights into what the problem might be, and none into what his own needs were, beyond pacifying Marie. His arrival at my office was an act of sheer desperation—on both their parts. Bill hoped that I could patch him up in a couple of sessions, and everything would be fine again.

To be honest, it looked pretty ominous. Bill was walking right into a war zone. He already had one foot over the line and didn't know it. He kept marching forward with his head up, praying life would somehow go back to the way it used to be—but it wouldn't. Even Marie didn't have very high hopes for the relationship. She really thought it was finished, and Bill couldn't see how close she was to dumping him.

Bill was a plain, ordinary, decent guy, and a great caretaker. He was just emotionally retarded.

We'll find out more about what happened to both Carol and Bill in the next chapter.

Chapter Two

Alone: The First Strange Feelings

I n this chapter, we'll concentrate on what you have to endure in the early days after separation—why you feel so terrible, and what you can do about it. We'll explore the connection between separation and mourning—grieving over a death—and why it's so important at this stage. Finally, we'll conclude the chapter with eight essential steps you can take to get yourself through this painful stage, and on to better times.

The next time Carol arrived for her appointment, she tripped coming into my office. Recovering her balance and her dignity, she mumbled something about a loose heel. She lowered herself delicately into her chair, as if fearful of breaking something. Her eyes were red and raw around the lids.

As we've seen, Carol was going through some difficulties with her husband, Richard. And yet, on previous occasions, she'd always managed to look well-groomed and elegant—ever the organized professional woman. This time, something had happened to Carol's facade: I'd never seen her so disheveled and fragile. Her expression was dazed, her posture stooped, her voice flat and inconsolable.

I asked her what had happened since our last talk.

"Richard went to the cottage for the long weekend," she began. "By himself. Said he had to be alone. He needed 'space' to do some 'serious thinking.' I said all right, I'd stay home and do stuff around the house. Mostly what I did was drink coffee all weekend and wait for him to come back and tell me what he was going to tell me."

She dabbed at the tear welling up in the corner of one eye.

"Sunday night, he got home late, said we had some talking to do. That means Richard talks, I listen. What it came down to is, he's very dissatisfied—with me, our sex life . . . everything. He's been terribly unhappy with our marriage for a very long time. He's waited for it to change; for me to change, to improve things. But, according to him, it hasn't happened.

"So." She shrugged helplessly. "Next day, he left. Just like that. Moved out. My Easter present. He's going to stay at a friend's until he finds his own place. He said I should go ahead and phone a lawyer—he even gave me a name to call."

Carol paused, staring at the wall, then at me. "I feel," she said, "like I'm going to die of a broken heart."

By the time she stopped crying, I was out of Kleenex.

Carol's story wasn't all that unusual. Literally thousands of people in our society break up with their spouses and partners every day. For many in their thirties and forties, it's become a virtual rite of passage.

But even as a hardened observer of such events, I couldn't help but feel touched by Carol's emotions. She was literally quite devastated by what had happened. It doesn't matter how many people you know who have gone through a marriage breakup before you—when it's happening to you, the effect is overwhelming. Nothing can prepare you adequately for the deep sadness of knowing that your familiar world has just been shattered.

Strangely enough, the impact can be equally powerful whether you're the one who gets left, or you're the one doing the leaving. The impact hits the one who is left sooner, of course. But it does eventually catch up with the one who leaves, as well. Nobody is immune from the emotional upheaval, the sheer, god-awful pain, of separation.

IN THE WAR ZONE

In the days and weeks that follow the split, you feel more alone than you've felt for a very long time. Like Carol, you're not only terribly sad and torn up inside—you feel frightened, too. Sometimes downright terrified.

You think: What's going to happen to me now? My God, I hadn't counted on *this*. This was never how I saw myself—vulnerable, exposed, confused. Weak. Helpless. Alone.

Even when reason tells us we're not really helpless, and there's no cause to feel afraid, we experience fear all the same: not constantly (that would be impossible to bear), but certainly more frequently than we'd like. In our most vulnerable moments, it comes sneaking up on us from behind, from that dark place where we've been hiding our worst fears ever since we were kids.

Sometimes you might feel as though you're staggering through a war zone. Bombs are falling, exploding all around you; even the ground seems to be mined. You don't know where it's safe to set foot, where you can find shelter. If that isn't bad enough, simultaneously a hurricane has blown up from nowhere, and you feel as if you're making headway in the fury of a hundred-mile-per-hour gale. You're constantly bracing yourself, battling along at a forty-five-degree angle, just to keep from getting knocked flat.

You wonder if all this turmoil is only temporary. How do you know it won't settle in and become permanent? That's a tough one to handle. Indeed, the uncertainty of this period, the seeming impossibility of predicting when—or if—life is going to improve, is often the scariest part of all.

These first unfamiliar feelings now assaulted Carol from all sides. She looked at me miserably, mute appeal in her eyes. Still, she offered no word of criticism of Richard, no anger at what he'd done or said—she passively accepted her fate, as if she actually deserved it. She was still too dazed, too shellshocked, to take any kind of action.

During the session, Carol told me something she'd only touched on previously: Richard had left her once before. It had happened three years earlier, and he'd been gone for six months. That had been a terrible time, too. But there had been one good thing about it, she said with a fleeting ghost of a smile—in Richard's absence she'd lost thirty pounds and had managed to keep them off ever since.

But Carol sensed there was something fundamentally different this time. This was it: Richard was gone for good. And all she could do was feel broken up about it.

For several minutes, she wistfully recalled some of the good things they'd shared: when they courted in college, and later, when they launched their marriage and careers with such high hopes, and Richard had helped her get ahead in the company. That was one area, at least, where he'd been supportive of her. He was always so superrational, Carol said admiringly: so totally in control of every situation. (How typical of Richard, I thought, to tell her which lawyer she should get to handle her side of the divorce!)

Everything between them had been fine, Carol believed, until they'd tried unsuccessfully to conceive a child five years ago. Attempting every fertility method going, they'd shared a sense of commitment and partnership, of working toward a common goal. But in the end, she had not become pregnant. The marriage had begun to slide downhill from there. After failing to conceive, it seemed she could do nothing right in Richard's eyes. It had been impossible to please him, no matter how hard she tried.

"So here I am, and it's all over," she said hoarsely. "I'm thirty-seven, on my own, with no idea where I'm going. It's probably too late to have kids. I have a decent job, but I'll never make vice-president. I have a few friends—mostly couples, people I met through Richard. The only ones I consider my personal friends have the cottage next to ours, and Richard says he loves the cottage so much he wants to keep it as part of the settlement! I just don't know what's going to happen to me."

Carol felt lost and desperate. Her anguish reminded me acutely of a bad time in my own life: the first Monday morning after my separation. I'd holed up in an apartment hotel downtown, and after a particularly unappetizing breakfast, I had gone down to the parking garage, got behind the wheel of my car and set out for the office. At the first big intersection, I stopped for a red light and watched all the busy people walking past in the sunshine on their way to work. They looked so *normal,* so brisk and cheery and healthy, and I thought: How can they do that? How can anybody function and smile and be happy this morning? Will *I* ever be that way again?

At such times, you feel so damaged inside that you can't believe the whole world isn't damaged. Other people seem to have it all together—why don't you? Their apparent self-confidence is a constant reprimand, a condemnation of what you've done to your life. Or so it seems.

I know how awful it feels; I've been there. I don't want to sugarcoat the pain, because it's all too real.

But I can tell you one thing: It doesn't last forever.

TIMETABLE TO RECOVERY

The first weeks immediately after separation are the worst. You feel as if you're in a deep, black pit—practically buried by your grief. This is survival time.

At this crucial stage, you have only one basic goal, and it's very straightforward: to live your life from day to day. If you can simply survive, one day at a time, you've achieved success for now. The rest can wait.

You are, in fact, playing a waiting game. You're waiting for the acute pain of your breakup to ebb away. Gradually, your disorientation will be replaced by a growing sense of autonomy and well-being, rooted in the new adult self you're creating, appropriate to the new circumstances of your life. That's the payoff. But for the time being, all you can do is tough it out.

This first stage typically lasts about three months—less for some people, longer for others. However long it lasts, just surviving from day to day must be your main concern.

Then, around three months after separation, you'll start looking out over the edges of your dark emotional pit. You'll feel a desire to know what's out there for you. Increasingly, you'll think about rejoining the world as a full participant, instead of remaining a bystander. This is the second stage. During the next several months, you'll make your first forays into the "outside world."

In the next stage—usually twelve to twenty-four months after separation—you'll follow up those forays by becoming more seriously involved with the people and activities that interest and attract you. The pain of your marriage breakup will begin to fade, even if it doesn't entirely disappear. You'll develop a clearer, sharper sense of yourself as a single person, an individual.

Finally, anywhere between two and three years after separation, your distinctive adult self will jell. You'll no longer feel like the damaged half of a broken marriage. You'll derive your unique identity from being a capable, competent, adult human being—separate but whole.

This timetable may seem arbitrary, but it corresponds to the actual recovery experience of the great majority of my patients, and many people like them. In all probability, it will become your experience too.

In this chapter, we'll deal only with the first stage: that deep, dark pit. We'll get to the other stages in later chapters.

So why does this stage feel so awful? Why is the pit so black? Why do you, a normal, intelligent human being, feel so afraid? The answer is precisely that you *are* a normal, intelligent human being, and your fearful reaction to what's happened is entirely appropriate.

Think, for a moment, about people who've been decorated for bravery in wartime or civilian life, who've been through hell and back, who've seen others killed and had their own lives thrust into mortal danger. In interviews or memoirs, practically every one of those brave, heroic individuals admits to being terrified at the time. Yet they carried on and did what they had to do—and survived.

Only the foolhardy have no fear. There are times when we *should* feel afraid, when fear is a perfectly legitimate and necessary response to a threat. A physical or medical emergency is one such time; a marriage breakup is another.

Alone after separation, you find that some of the most fundamental props of your existence have been knocked out from under you. It's natural to feel afraid: After years of marriage or living together, you're not sure how to survive in the unknown territory of single men and women. Actually, it's necessary to feel that way—just as it's necessary to walk at a strange angle to keep from getting blown over by a hurricane.

Being afraid doesn't mean you're inadequate. It means you're preparing yourself for the main task that lies ahead in the next few weeks and months: survival.

A TIME TO MOURN

Even when you put fear in its place, however, you can't get around the sadness set in motion by the end of a relationship. Where does this sadness come from? Carol felt sad because she wanted her marriage to continue. But even people who *want* their relationships to end, knowing it's for the best, feel desperately sad when it actually happens. Why?

A patient of mine, whom I'll call Linda, summed it up perfectly. When Linda came in to talk about her three-week-long separation from her husband, Stan, she said: "Our relationship is going through its death throes."

A highly skilled and pragmatic registered nurse, Linda knew what she was talking about. "It's just like having a patient die in intensive care," she told me. "After a certain point, there's nothing more you can do but watch." Linda had seen many patients die, after everything humanly possible had been done for them. Now she was watching her marriage die.

Once you understand that the end of a marriage is truly a death, certain things become clearer, more comprehensible: for instance, the times when you feel overwhelmed by grief; when you burst into tears in public; when you feel the emotional emptiness as a sharp physical pain gnawing at your insides like an ulcer; when you forget appointments or lose your car keys, awash in a general state of disorganization, because your grief is like a flood sweeping aside the relatively minor details of existence.

None of this behavior would seem strange coming from a person who was in mourning, grieving over the loss of a beloved parent or child. If you noticed a colleague at work, who had just lost his mother to cancer, staring off blankly into space, or weeping silently in the middle of the work day, you'd immediately understand and accept the reason. You wouldn't consider your colleague weak, foolish, abnormal, or crazy. Such behavior would seem a natural response to one of life's harshest blows.

During and after the death of your marriage, you can extend to yourself the same understanding and acceptance. You too are in mourning: After all, you've just suffered the death of one of the primary relationships of your life.

Like other states of mourning, this one will eventually come to an end. Life, while irrevocably changed, will go back to "normal." In the meantime, it's normal to grieve; if you act a little strange, accept that it's just part of the grieving process.

The parallel between the grief of mourning and the grief of divorce struck me forcibly right after the end of my own marriage. At the time, I was afraid I'd find it unbearably painful to treat patients who were experiencing marital problems—but I didn't. Instead, I felt torn apart by four other patients, all of whom were simultaneously grieving over the recent or imminent death of a loved one. These men and women were living through the same kind of acute grief that I was: We were *all* in mourning, all lamenting a death—only in my case, it was the death of a relationship. Until then, I'd never realized the close connection between separation and mourning.

LINDA'S STORY

In the case of my patient Linda, it was her husband, Stan, who left the marriage. But ironically, it was Linda who recovered from the breakup first.

There was no other person involved, no marriage-breaking fight, no dramatic catalyst to explain why Stan moved out after a seven-year relationship. One day, without warning, he simply told Linda he'd taken an apartment. When she asked why, he admitted he wasn't entirely sure of his reasons, only that he "had to"—a compulsion he didn't feel able to resist.

At first, Linda was angry. For the previous eighteen months, she'd repeatedly tried to get Stan to sit down and talk about their life together. She knew their relationship was in difficulty. Things weren't horribly wrong between them; they just weren't horribly right, either.

Linda believed that if only she and Stan could talk, they'd sort it out somehow. After all, they were reasonable and fair-minded people. But Stan always shied away from confronting the issues in the relationship, citing work pressures or fatigue (women aren't the only ones to say, "Not tonight, dear, I'm too tired"), or simply denying there were any problems to deal with. Linda believed their relationship had to change in order to survive, but Stan stubbornly resisted change. And now here he was, declaring without consultation that he couldn't handle staying together any longer.

Linda's anger at Stan was followed by a profound sadness. When she told me her marriage was "going through its death throes," they'd been living apart for three weeks. Stan had invited her for dinner at his new place on a Friday evening, and she'd found him in a shaky, fragile state. He was nearly distraught, full of regrets and remorse and confusion, but still planning to live apart from her.

"This has been the worst week of my life," he told Linda. "If only I could take back the things I said when I told you I was moving out." He went on in that vein, covering the well-trodden ground of "if only" and "might have": If only they'd done this or that differently, everything might have been different.

Linda listened, hearing the panic and fear in Stan's voice. All the time, her own sadness and pain were growing inside her. That was when she diagnosed the relationship as not merely ill, but terminal. She'd already lived through one marriage breakup, and she recognized the signs.

Linda's first marriage had been sick in a very different way. Her first husband was an alcoholic who had abused her physically, and she'd left him and taken the two children after a beating one night twelve years ago. Certainly she'd been more frightened then than she was now. Yet she was sadder this time. Stan had always been a really nice guy; in fact, now he was saying he wanted them to be "friends," and to still see each other now and again.

Linda knew this wasn't possible for her—at least not for a while.

Perhaps it would be possible later, after her grieving for her dead marriage was over. But for now, realist that she was, she had to let this relationship with Stan die first before she could make another one with him.

He found her attitude coldhearted. "How can you be so hard?" he had asked in tears.

"What he wouldn't see was that I was falling apart inside," Linda told me. "He had no concept of what I was going through."

Stan wanted Linda's forgiveness and approval. That way, he wouldn't have to take responsibility for his own actions—much like a teenager who leaves home, then asks his parents for money to live on. Stan was frightened by what he'd done. He was surprised by how much it cost him emotionally to leave his marriage, yet he had a lot of trouble accepting the price. He really wanted Linda to kiss his wounds and make them all better.

For her part, Linda came to grips with the reality far more quickly than Stan. She knew she'd survive this: She'd survived the death of a marriage before, and she could do it again. But she also knew she'd have to face the pain first. She'd have to mourn the death of a relationship in which she'd invested seven years of her life.

Because he wouldn't acknowledge his pain, it took Stan a lot longer to mourn the death of his marriage, and thus become free to begin a new life. The fact is, there's no way around the suffering; nothing will make it better instantly. People often delude themselves into thinking that if they move out on their own, or run off with the ski instructor, their lives will be much better. It isn't that easy.

Marriages may end in a thousand different ways, but there is one verity when a marriage dies, one consequence that's always the same for both partners: It hurts like hell.

THE CARPET ANALOGY

What happens when you *don't* mourn your dead relationship? Well, it won't be fatal, and you may even avoid some sadness or depression for a while; but sooner or later you'll experience certain consequences. Some of them are described in the next chapter, "Ten Common Pitfalls for the Newly Separated." In the meantime, here's an analogy to illustrate the general problem:

Let's say your boss is coming over for a visit on short notice, and you're rushing around your place to tidy it up. You've swept the dirt, crumbs, and fur balls into a nice neat pile, but she's going to arrive any second, so you sweep the pile temporarily under the carpet for safekeeping. Fine.

But, comparable to the issues and feelings you have to deal with in divorce, suppose there's a whole big mess of things to sweep up. If you hide all of that stuff under the carpet, you'll have an enormous mound of debris protruding from the living room floor. And if you won't acknowledge that it's there, you're going to have problems. The next time you walk through your living room, you might trip over that great lump of debris whose existence you're denying, and fall flat on your face. So why did you fall? Since you've ruled out the idea that there is a pile of stuff under the carpet, there has to be some other explanation. Good Lord, maybe you have fainting spells, or multiple sclerosis, or a brain tumor—or even dropsy!

If you acknowledged the mess, at least you'd have a comprehensible reason for your fall. But without that acknowledgment, you can jump to false conclusions that can actually cause worse problems—all quite unnecessarily.

In the wake of your separation, you can make the same mistake of ignoring or denying the death of your relationship, and refusing to grieve over it. Yet you wonder why you feel so terrible. You may draw false conclusions, such as, "If I feel this bad, I must still love him (or her). If I go back, I'll feel better." So you return to an unsatisfactory or deeply flawed relationship instead of mourning its passing and making a better life.

It's better to grieve for what you've lost, as you would for any other death. Embrace your sadness. Express it—along with your other inevitable feelings, such as disappointment, bitterness, anger—to yourself and others. Then you'll have a better chance of getting over it all, and eventually getting on with your life. When you don't mourn, you risk misinterpreting what your feelings are really about.

BUILD ON YOUR STRENGTHS

It's understandable that you'd rather not have to go through some of your feelings surrounding the death of your relationship. They aren't pleasant. What if you don't have the strength to handle it?

Well, you do. At this point, it's a very good idea to remind yourself of some of the strengths you've developed during the course of your life, strengths you can rely on to get you through this dark period.

I had a patient, Sara, who was terrified at the outset of her separation. She felt unequal to the task of rebuilding her life.

Sara told me: "All I've ever wanted was to be a wife and mother—to help my husband and raise my kids. Sure, I worked for several years as a flight attendant. But my goal was never to have a wonderful career for its own sake. It was to make some money to help build a life for me and Lyle and the kids.

"Even when Lyle's business was in trouble, I pitched in gladly and kept the books for a year, so he wouldn't have to pay a book-keeper. The company almost went bankrupt, but between us we managed to save it. And even though our family savings got wiped out, it felt good to pull together and come through. It was all right, because we were building something.

"But *now* what do I do? Where am I supposed to go from here? I don't know what's going to happen to me or the kids. Lyle and I always tried to provide for their dance lessons and figure-skating lessons and what have you, but I can't afford it anymore. We may even have to move; they'll lose their friends. I've spent my whole adult life building in this one direction and now it's all gone. Honestly, I'm beginning to panic."

Sara was afraid, and she had a right to be. But she had forgotten some important facts about herself. She forgot she'd had a career before, and she could have one again. She forgot she was president of the PTA at her kids' school; the other parents had elected her because they respected her as a capable, competent adult, with skills and personal qualities they admired. She forgot how much strength and resourcefulness she'd demonstrated when she stepped in to help save her husband's business from bankruptcy.

In her panic, Sara had lost sight of those strengths. So we went over them together. She remembered all the times she'd faced adversity in the past and had overcome it. She could do it again. She recalled her father's death when she was seventeen, how frightened and overwhelmed she'd felt, how she hadn't known what was going to happen to her and her mother; eventually she'd mourned her father's passing and accepted it. She could do it again.

At that point, I couldn't predict how everything was going to turn out for Sara, any more than she could. But I could acknowledge with her how scared she felt. I could help her look back and recognize her strengths and capabilities. They were her ace in the hole; they were going to allow her to climb up out of her deep, dark pit and, once again, come into the light. That much I could predict—and I turned out to be right.

EIGHT ESSENTIAL STEPS FOR SURVIVING DAY TO DAY

Your basic goal in this first stage of separation is to survive from day to day. The way to reach that goal is to look after yourself—legally, financially, physically, and emotionally.

After years of living with someone, of sharing daily routines and obligations, you might have fallen out of the habit of taking sole responsibility for the one person you're uniquely qualified to look after: *yourself*. Here are some simple guidelines for performing that vital task. These eight steps may seem elementary, but they're essential for ensuring your success in passing through the survival stage, and for building the foundations of your new adult self that will later emerge.

Step 1: See a Lawyer

The importance of obtaining professional legal advice can't be overestimated. Seek out a specialist in family law. Ask friends, relatives, or colleagues (especially those who have been through a divorce) if they can recommend a good family lawyer. Seek a referral from the lawyer who helped you buy your house. Failing that, the bar association in your area will be able to provide you with a list of family lawyers practicing close by.

The purpose of your first visit to a lawyer is not to arrive at final terms for a separation agreement or divorce settlement, but simply to clarify your rights under the law. A lawyer can be extremely helpful in letting you know if you're being fair in your expectations and demands—most of all, if you're being fair to yourself. At this time, you need to look after yourself in every sense, including the legal sense.

Some people feel reluctant to seek out legal advice. Are there situations where it's better *not* see a lawyer?

The answer is no—never. Even if you want to keep the door open to a reconciliation with your spouse, it's still important to know your rights. Otherwise, you're putting yourself at a serious disadvantage. If you still hope to reconcile, tell that to your lawyer, instruct him or her not to pursue a settlement just yet, and especially not to represent you in a belligerent fashion with your spouse's lawyer. Your lawyer's job is to serve your interests.

Use the first visit to ascertain your legal rights and reasonable expectations regarding division of property and assets, support payments, child custody and access, and any other matters that concern you. Ask what the lawyer thinks he or she can do for you, given your situation, and roughly how much it's likely to cost. Most conscientious lawyers are willing to sit down with you and answer these kinds of questions in an exploratory first session for a reasonable fee—sometimes even for no fee.

I realize it can sometimes be tough to take this step. When you walk into a lawyer's office, you are leaping over a psychological hurdle. It makes your marriage breakup seem all the more concrete; to expose your personal life to strangers is to acknowledge a bitter, painful reality. But it *is* a reality—hence it's all the more important to come to grips with its legal and financial side. If you know a hurricane is on its way, you close the shutters, board up the windows and doors, batten the hatches, and stow the sails. Going to see a lawyer is like that: a sensible precaution.

Remember, too, the old adage: Whoever acts as his own counsel has a fool for a client. A third party generally does the best job of representing your interests. The best illustration of what a lawyer can do for you comes from a friend of mine. Asked to recommend a good divorce lawyer, he cheerfully named his ex-wife's counsel, saying: "He took me for everything I was worth!"

Nonetheless, if, after understanding your rights, you and your spouse can reach a fair agreement about division of assets, child support, and so forth, you may minimize time and expense (which are closely related in legal matters) by asking one lawyer to review and expedite your agreement from the viewpoint of both your interests.

Step 2: Plan Your Finances

One of the first things a lawyer will ask you to do is to complete a detailed statement of your monthly income and expenses. This is essential in determining how much money you'll need each month to survive, and whether you're going to have enough. Even if you haven't visited a lawyer yet, it's important to do this calculation. There is inevitably far less money to go around after a couple has split into two households. Looking after yourself means ensuring you have at least the minimum financial security to sustain you until a separation or divorce agreement is reached.

This means having enough income to meet the basic needs of daily living: your accommodation, food, clothing, utilities, and child care expenses, if applicable. Actual needs will vary, depending on your existing life-style and whether you have dependent children or a job. Whatever your circumstances, be as comprehensive, practical, and realistic as you can in writing down your monthly expenses and income. That way, you'll know just where you are financially and can act accordingly.

Lawyers are not financial planners, but they can advise you on what you should be thinking about. I'm not a financial planner either, but I'll mention a couple of important principles that apply to everyone, whether you're a husband or wife, wage earner or homemaker, young adult or pensioner.

There are two serious mistakes that recently separated people make when it comes to financial settlements. One is to surrender their financial rights by saying, "Don't worry, I want nothing from you," or "Oh, I don't care, you take everything."

This can be a huge mistake. Not only would you be abdicating your legal and moral rights, but you'd also be leaving yourself vulnerable to severe financial hardship in the future.

I had a patient, Joan, whose husband, Tim, left her and their three children for a woman living five doors up the street. Joan was not only bereaved but utterly furious: "I never liked that floozie anyway, and now I know why. If he's going to carry on with her, fine—I want nothing more to do with him. I never want to see him again, and I sure as hell don't want to owe him anything. I'll go on social assistance before I'll accept a red cent from him. Anything, as long as he won't bother us!"

I told Joan her fury was understandable. But I had to talk her out of rejecting financial support for herself and the children. Tim's behavior was deeply hurtful to her, but it had nothing to do with the settlement she should seek. Her attitude was a form of self-mutilation; she was hurting only herself.

First, she was giving up her legal rights to some of the assets of the marriage. Second, she was trying to make a trade-off between money and access to the kids, thinking she could refuse Tim access if she also refused to take his support. All in all, she was being unfair to herself, to Tim, and to the children, who had a right to see their father on a regular basis. Joan ultimately saw my point. Her reaction illustrates the self-defeating behavior that's possible when people try to act out their emotions.

A male patient, Terry, had already made his mistake—in writing—before he came to see me. Terry had felt so guilty over breaking up his marriage that he'd signed away his rights to his fair share of the joint assets. "I felt so rotten, I told her she could have it all—the house, the car, the RV, the boat, the kids. I thought it would make me feel better. Now I wish I could do it all over again. It's going to take me years to dig myself out of poverty."

The other big mistake is to blindly trust a spouse's word about support payments, or division of assets, without getting it down in writing. You need more assurance than that: You need a written agreement about how much money you'll get, on what date, and in what form—cash, certified check, postdated checks. You need a binding agreement you can count on, or, if necessary, fall back on in court, even before the separation agreement or divorce settlement is finalized. The rent or mortgage payments, grocery bills, or child-care expenses aren't going to stop just because your marriage has broken up; you need to know how they're going to get paid.

These are the opening financial moves that will help you obtain an early modicum of security in an insecure situation. The final, long-term financial settlement will come later.

Step 3: Let People Know

Even though you may find it painful or embarrassing, there are some good practical reasons why you should let people know about your separation. It's better to clarify the situation instead of hiding it. It helps avoid misunderstandings. Most of all, it helps you to accept your new situation, and to get on familiar terms with it.

The people you should tell include friends, family members, colleagues, and co-workers. Tell them in a simple, direct, even clinical manner. You don't need to go into all the details or reasons at first.

As you tell people, you'll get a good sense of which ones feel supportive toward you, just by the way they respond to your news. Not everyone will be supportive, but most will; stay in contact with those who are. In a time of crisis, you need support and understanding more than anything. Don't hesitate to ask for it.

Seeking people's understanding isn't a sign of weakness or unworthiness. People will respect you for being up-front about needing to talk. You have to trust that your friends will be there for you, just as you'd be there for them if the tables were turned. In an emergency like this, you find out who your real friends are.

If a friend or relative acts cold or unresponsive, however, don't be too upset. Your news may make them feel uncomfortable, even threatened. This probably has more to do with their own lives and marriages than with yours. They may simply need time to get used to the idea that you and your spouse won't be together anymore.

Inevitably, a few people will take sides. Some will be more supportive of you than of your ex, while others may conclude that your ex is a fine person and you're a dirty rotten swine. Still others will try to be equally supportive of both of you. You can't always predict how people will react, or count on them all to respond in the same way.

How to tell people? There are different methods. Friends of mine who separated mailed out announcements—"Dan and Donna wish to let their friends know they have reached an amicable decision to go their separate ways"—a kind of reverse wedding announcement. I threw a housewarming party at my new apartment for friends and colleagues; anyone who didn't know about my separation soon found out.

More typically, you may want to make a list of all the friends and relatives who should know about the breakup, and call them on the phone. In the process, you can make arrangements for lunch or dinner with those to whom you really want to pour your heart out.

You have a right to expect your friends to be there for you. One small caveat, however: It's better not to depend on any one friend for all the sympathy you need. To do so would be to overburden him or her. Instead, share yourself around. If you have, say, four friends, and you arrange to visit a different one each week, that means you've turned to each of them just once a month.

There's one other advantage in talking with many different people. The process is similar to the mourning rituals of the funeral parlor, or to the Jewish custom of sitting *shiva* in memory of a loved one. With every person who shares your mourning, you get to tell the story of the death all over again. This is very useful, because it makes the event more real for you; each retelling provides a fresh perspective on what happened, a new insight or consolation, allowing you to make greater sense of the death of your relationship, and to move beyond it.

Step 4: Set a Place for Yourself at the Table
At this time, some people feel so upset and disoriented they forget to eat. I never recommend starvation for the person recovering from marriage breakup.

Sure, it's not as much fun eating by yourself, or preparing a meal for one. If you have kids, it can be tempting just to fix them some kid food—hot dogs or a Kraft dinner or frozen pizza—and not bother to sit down and eat anything yourself. Anyway, there's that knot in the pit of your stomach, which seems to be taking the place of food. But starving yourself can lead to worse problems: loss of energy and stamina, just when you need them most—not to mention malnutrition if you take things too far. Likewise, grazing the entire contents of the refrigerator every evening is also harmful.

Be sure to set a place for yourself at the table. Sit down and feed the body (in moderation) as well as the soul.

If you haven't had much experience in the kitchen, ask a friend or relative for guidance. A book such as *Joy of Cooking* will tell you exactly what to do with carrots or onions or lamb chops. It contains explicit instructions for anyone who doesn't know a colander from a Cuisinart, or for anyone who is afraid to turn on the stove and raise the temperature of objects in a pan.

My patient Harvey, for instance, couldn't boil water. He'd been married for fifteen years and had four kids at the time he separated from his wife. One of Harvey's biggest problems was that he'd never done any of the cooking at home, yet he wanted to have his kids come and visit him regularly. How was he going to feed them? He couldn't afford to take them to restaurants every time. Besides, he wanted them to regard his new apartment as their second home, and that meant making it a place where they could get a decent meal.

Harvey knew where to come for advice. (Somehow he'd divined

that, whereas some people eat to live, his psychiatrist lives to eat.)
He and I sat down and worked out one week's sample menu. To
get him started, I wrote out some simple recipes for dishes he
could cook right away, and suggested a few good cookbooks.

Harvey went away determined to succeed. A year later, he'd become a far better cook than I am: He was making gourmet meals for
his family and friends. Now Harvey likes to excel at whatever he
does (he's also very good at squash and neurosurgery); his approach
to cooking contained a strong element of pride. He didn't want to
remain in a state of incompetence and dependency regarding something as important as eating. An inability to cook is not, in the end,
sufficient reason to stay in a bad marriage. And while not everyone
wants to go to the extremes Harvey did, this example shows how
much can be accomplished by starting with a few simple recipes.

Step 5: Get a Good Night's Sleep

In the acute phase of the grieving process, it's fairly common to
have difficulty sleeping. This can mean difficulty falling asleep in
the first place, or interruption of sleep from waking frequently during the night.

Different people need different amounts of sleep. You have to
determine how much your sleep disturbances are interfering with
your ability to function during the day. If the disturbances are
interfering significantly, causing serious loss of energy and concentration, then you might consider obtaining some sleep medication
from your doctor, to use only when necessary.

To avoid becoming dependent on the medication, it's wise to
take it every third night at most. That way, you can at least be
sure of getting a decent night's sleep now and again. You'll have
to make your own judgment on this point. If you're getting only
two or three hours' sleep every night, you can't go on like that;
it's important to be able to function as well as possible. But if, a
couple of nights a week, you find yourself wide awake until three
in the morning, tossing and turning and worrying about money or
the kids, that's normal and to be expected at this stage. In that
case, a glass of warm milk and a banana (to make up a possible
deficiency of the neurotransmitter serotonin, which the body pro-
duces) may do the trick.

Step 6: Make a Comfortable Nest

Along with eating and sleeping properly, another important way to look after yourself is to take care of your physical surroundings. You deserve a nice place in which to live. Even if it's not the Taj Mahal, why shouldn't it have clean walls, comfortable furniture, and attractive curtains or drapes? You're going to be spending a lot of time in your home; that time will be more pleasant if your surroundings are pleasant, too.

This may be a less pressing matter if you're staying in the home you've occupied for some time. But if you're establishing a new residence, it takes on a fundamental importance.

If you're inexperienced at painting, decorating, picking out furniture, or putting up curtains, you can seek help. Ask advice from people who know about these things: a professional painter or decorator. It will cost some money, but if you can afford it, it's worth it. If you can't afford it, collect decorating tips and ideas from friends, and use the ones you like.

Your friends may also be willing to pitch in and help with big jobs like moving furniture, painting walls, or hanging wallpaper. Reach out and ask them. Make a fun evening or Saturday afternoon out of it by supplying food and drink.

You must remember that you're looking after yourself now. If you don't do it, nobody else will. You're not totally on your own, but naturally friends will feel more inclined to help if they see you helping yourself. Put yourself in their position: Suppose you're driving along a country road and you see a car stuck in the ditch. The driver has his feet up on the steering wheel, saying "Push me!" Would you be inclined to stop and push? But if the driver was actively doing his best to get himself out of the ditch, you'd feel more sympathetic, and more like lending a hand.

Now is the time to start doing things for yourself, to show yourself and others that you're well worth the effort. You may not believe this now, but in six months or a year, things will look a whole lot better to you—just how much better depends a great deal on what you do now.

Step 7: Treat Yourself to Something Nice

What would be nice for you? To spend an afternoon at the art gallery or the ball game? To go for a long bike ride? To invite some friends for dinner? To buy some flowers for the mantelpiece, or a chunk of brie and a baguette? To set aside time to garden or read a good book?

Whatever you enjoy doing, now's the time to do it. When you were married, maybe there was never enough time for your favorite activities and enthusiasms. Maybe your spouse didn't enjoy them as much as you do. Maybe the two of you got into routines—ruts, really—that somehow omitted the things that are special to you and you alone. Somehow, your wishes had a way of coming last on the list.

Well, not any more. Now they come first. Even if you think it's a bit self-indulgent, go ahead and do the things you like to do. You're worth it.

When I was first separated and staying in the apartment hotel, I went around and looked at apartments, trying to imagine myself living in one of them. The only one I really liked was a nicely furnished little place with a charming bedroom and balcony. Trouble was, the rent was just a little more than my lawyer and I had calculated I could afford. On the other hand, since the place was furnished, I wouldn't have to spend money for furniture or drapes. I phoned my lawyer, who's also a friend, and explained my dilemma. He proved he was a friend by saying, "Go for it!" He was right. That pleasant apartment made life so much more enjoyable that it boosted my morale and speeded my recovery. It was well worth the cost.

So indulge yourself now and then. Some of life's pleasures don't even cost a cent. You're free to enjoy them now, to do the things that are only for you. Take advantage of your freedom. You'll find it makes you feel better about being alive.

Step 8: Be Straight with the Kids

In later chapters, especially in Chapter 6, I'll be talking about your relationships with your children, if any. For now, here are several considerations to keep in mind at this stage: some simple but essential things to know and do regarding your kids at the beginning of your separation.

1. In straightforward, concrete terms appropriate to their age and maturity levels, tell them clearly what's happening. Don't lie about the fact that Mommy and Daddy are separating. Evading

the truth by saying Mommy or Daddy is "going away on a trip" is unnecessary, possibly damaging, and certainly unfair to your children. They have a right to know the truth about something so important to them.

2. Reassure them that, even though Mommy and Daddy are separating, you still love them. Mommy still loves them and Daddy still loves them. And Mommy will always be their mommy, just as Daddy will always be their daddy. Put it in those exact absolute terms: *always*. Kids need some absolute certainties right now, when life seems to have become so uncertain.

3. Children, especially young ones, have a tendency to see themselves as the cause of whatever happens around them: They regard themselves as *causal*. Therefore, it's important to reassure them that the separation is not their fault; that something has gone wrong between Mommy and Daddy, and it's nothing they did.

4. It's time to put an end to the idea that children of "broken homes" (in that old-fashioned, moralizing phrase) turn out badly. But just how they turn out will be influenced by how you and your spouse handle the separation. For example, it's vital to try and ensure regular, consistent, dependable contact between the children and the noncustodial parent. This won't be a problem if you and your spouse have agreed that the kids should spend equal time with both of you. But if they're living with one parent only, the other parent should be able to see them at specified, predictable times. Research has shown that such regular contact has very positive long-term effects on children; they turn out emotionally healthier and more secure. And it facilitates relations between ex-spouses on practical issues of custody and support payments.

5. Don't bad-mouth your ex-spouse to the kids. No matter how angry, bitter, or vengeful you feel toward your ex, he or she is still the children's parent. Did you ever like anyone bad-mouthing your mom or dad, even though your parents were far from perfect? It's tempting to point out your ex's failings to the kids, but doing so just makes a hard time harder for them. They shouldn't be made to suffer for the inadequacies of your marriage.

BILL'S STORY

I'll conclude this chapter by continuing the story of Bill, whom we met at the end of Chapter 1. When he came into my office to talk about his separation, Bill put it this way: "Well, Marie has decided we'd better split up. She has a lot of complaints—I spend way too much time working, I don't care enough about the kids—but hell, Doctor, nothing could be further from the truth. You know that—you know how much I love them.

"Anyway, she says she's had enough; she's been to see a lawyer and I've got to go. So I moved out on the weekend. I mean, Marie can have the house and the cottage. They're both so important to the kids, and I don't want to upset them. So I've rented a little one-bedroom apartment. It's kind of tacky, but what the hell, it's furnished, and it's near the store, and it's close enough to home that I can still pick the kids up and take them to their lessons and practices and stuff."

The gist of Bill's news was that he'd abdicated his rights to practically everything in his marriage except his duties as a provider and caretaker. There was nothing in this deal for him personally: He just worked. He was a drone, a money machine, a chauffeur. His wife and kids could keep everything, while he'd go on paying the bills and supplying rides.

"I told Marie: I may be no saint, but damn it all, I've always done my best to provide. Marie can keep all her charge cards. All she has to do is let me know how much things are costing, and I'll pay for them."

I wondered where Bill's feelings were in all this. When I asked him, he replied: "Oh, I don't know . . . as long as the kids are all right, I guess that's what matters. Of course, I'll have to keep up two places now. I'll just work a little harder building up sales at the store. I'll keep it all under control."

Bill wasn't doing his grieving. A few days earlier, he'd been kicked out of his own home, and he was showing neither grief nor anger.

"What have you been doing since you left?" I asked him.

"Oh, not a hell of a lot . . . besides putting in time at work. I'm not one for cooking or eating alone, so I've taken my meals at The Chances R, down the road from the store. Steak and pie, mostly. Oh, and I guess I've had quite a load to drink in the past few days. But you know, it's not much fun going back to a . . . well, it's a nice enough apartment, I suppose, I can't really complain . . . but it's a pretty dead place in the middle of the night. I'm not sleeping much, to tell the truth.

"Anyway, I've just got to carry on. That's all I can do. That, and try to make sure things are okay for the kids. Boy, were they upset when they saw me leaving. I don't know why it got to them so much."

In addition to abdicating his rights, Bill was abdicating responsibility for his feelings. He was letting his wife make the decisions and was totally ignoring his own needs.

I tried to reflect with him on how he was feeling about all this. He must be pretty upset, I suggested, because he was drinking far more than usual, and he wasn't sleeping. He also admitted he wasn't seeing a lawyer. This showed he was behaving very irrationally indeed; it meant he was denying the existence of some very real problems.

But the person Bill really had to take care of was himself. Although it was natural for him to have so much concern for his children, he also had to show more concern for his own needs and welfare. Part of looking after the children's interests right then was looking after himself. He wouldn't be much good to them if he let himself become a basket case.

I went over with Bill the above eight steps for surviving from day to day. In later chapters, we'll see how he managed.

Chapter Three

Ten Common Pitfalls for the Newly Separated

Newly separated people can stumble into a variety of pitfalls during the first months of being on their own again. If you should recognize yourself in any of these situations—if, in other words, you've already made some of these mistakes—don't be too surprised: they're entirely normal. You're human, after all. No one says you have to be "perfect," whatever that means. I always urge patients not to be too hard on themselves during the first hundred days after separation. If you're only at Day Twenty-seven or Day Sixty-four, you shouldn't be surprised if you encounter problems now and then.

In fact, I don't know anyone who hasn't experienced one or more of these pitfalls in the course of separating and divorcing. But it helps to know they're out there. It's like keeping your eyes peeled for that garden rake that once came up and hit you in the face: Once you're on the lookout for it, it's easier to avoid it.

In moderation, none of these tendencies has to lead to disaster. It's only when taken to excess that they can do any serious damage.

1. THE REBOUND RELATIONSHIP

When all of a sudden you find yourself "falling in love" with the first person who's nice to you after your separation—someone who offers affection, or even just a sympathetic ear or a willing hand—you're probably into the rebound relationship. While it may prove lasting in some cases, most often the rebound relationship is built on fleeting needs and temporary foundations.

Barbara was a woman who exemplified this pitfall in classic fashion. Just over forty when her husband left her, Barbara felt crushed by the collapse of her marriage. She hadn't worked outside the home since the birth of her first child. Now she had three teenage children to support and no income, apart from the monthly payments from her ex-husband. Barbara couldn't see how she was going to cope financially—quite apart from coping emotionally, which was overwhelming enough without the extra burden of money worries.

Three months after her separation, Barbara met a man. He behaved wonderfully toward her—he was so kind and considerate and understanding. And he'd make a wonderful dad for the children, Barbara decided. After dating him for ten weeks, she agreed to marry him.

He moved in with her after the wedding. That was just what Barbara wanted: a man in the house again; the continuity for the kids that a home and a two-parent family would provide. It was only then that she and her new husband got down to discussing practical issues.

He told Barbara he was going to keep his finances separate from hers. That seemed reasonable enough. But then he announced that he was prepared to contribute fifty dollars a week to the household expenses, period. That represented his share, he calculated, of the groceries he'd consume, plus his proportion of the household overhead as one out of five people living under the same roof.

On top of this miserly attitude, he became exceedingly jealous of Barbara's close relationships with her children. His interactions with the teenagers rapidly deteriorated into that of a bullying overlord. Eventually, he adopted the same stance toward Barbara herself; on one occasion, he actually assaulted her.

Instead of a wonderful father for her family, Barbara ended up with a brutal, jealous, penny-pinching tyrant. After eighteen months of a dreadful marriage, she finally got up the courage to divorce him.

In retrospect, Barbara realized that her horrendous mistake of rushing into this marriage arose from her emotional neediness at the time—especially her need to feel looked after. She'd been seeking a father figure, and not only for her kids. Now she's learned to look after herself. It's the best protection against going too far in the rebound relationship.

Incidentally, women aren't the only ones who rush into marriage to reestablish the pretense of a family. A female colleague recently told me about placing an ad in the personals column of the newspaper to find some interesting male companionship. After careful screening, she dated three different men, all of them nice guys. But two of them, she discovered, were separated fathers with custody, who were really looking for a mother for their kids—and themselves. They thought they were doing it for their children; in fact, they were projecting onto the kids their own need to be dependent and taken care of. We'll look more closely at that need in the next chapter.

All this is not to say that rebound relationships can't be beneficial. In the deep, black pit you fall into after separation, when you're hurting badly, it's natural to feel powerfully drawn toward the first caring, nurturing person you come across. At such a time, we all need extra nurturing. It isn't necessary to deny yourself a nurturing relationship—but it isn't necessary to marry the person either!

As time goes by, and you feel stronger and more able to manage on your own, the rebound relationship may appear a lot different to you. You may realize you don't want to make it permanent. Frances, for example, fell into a lesbian relationship with a friend she had met while attending a women's consciousness-raising group. This woman was the first warmly caring individual Frances had come across after separating from her husband. But six months later, Frances decided she had to move on, now that she had regained her self-confidence and could see more clearly what she wanted from life. Soon she began a heterosexual relationship, reflecting her primary sexual orientation. Her female lover felt rejected and hurt, and Frances lost a good friend.

The rebound relationship can be understood through the idea of the "transitional object." This concept comes from child psychology and goes like this: Around the age of two, we begin to enter the big, threatening world outside of Mother's love and protection, and it scares the hell out of us. In our anxiety, we literally hang onto a transitional object: something that makes us feel better because it provides a sense of safety and security. It might be a favorite teddy bear, a frayed blanket, or whatever. The exact nature of the transitional object doesn't matter, as long as it is associated with safety and helps us get over the bridge into early childhood.

So it can be with adults. After separation, we're again going through a major transition in our lives—entering the unknown—which threatens us and makes us feel anxious. We often latch onto that first sympathetic person on the rebound, in our efforts to regain a sense of emotional safety. We may even attribute virtues to that person, and to the relationship, which aren't truly there. Our desperate need for security temporarily overrides all other considerations.

Another problem with the rebound relationship arises from the "transitional object's" point of view. If you're using someone to get through a painful transition, then you're really dealing with that person as if he or she were an object, not a person. Looking at the relationship in that light helps you to view it more realistically, and to handle it more honestly and constructively. You can admit that just because the relationship is serving your needs right now, it doesn't have to last forever; and you can give your friend credit for being a person with needs of his or her own, and not an inanimate teddy bear.

Admittedly, one of your friend's needs may be to find someone to nurture, and that may be what attracted you to him or her in the first place. But not everyone feels that way. In singles groups, for example, it's commonplace to hear the veterans say of a new arrival: "He's a lovely guy, but he's too recently separated." What they mean is that he's too hurt, too needy, to get deeply involved with just yet.

Let me tell a story about myself. Just a couple of weeks after I separated, I was invited to a party. There I met a very charming, intelligent woman with whom I spent much of the evening chatting. One of her most charming qualities, I realize now, was her willingness to listen to me pour my heart out about my troubles. Afterward, she invited me back to her place for a nightcap, and we sat outside on her porch until the wee hours, talking.

In the end, she told me, "You're a fine fellow, Keith. But you're too recently separated to consider going out with."

For her, I was too raw emotionally—too needy—because I was hurting too much. She wasn't prepared to do the nurturing I needed right then. She implied that if I wanted to call her in two or three months, when I was feeling more together, then maybe we could see about taking it from there. And somehow she said it all kindly enough to let me down gently.

This woman was experienced enough to be warned off by the signals I was sending out, loud and clear. She wasn't about to become my transitional object in a rebound relationship.

2. THE WRONG FACE

There's usually a price to pay for getting intimately involved with someone who is not only your rebound relationship, but highly inappropriate for you as well, for one reason or another. It could be your boss, your best friend's wife, your sister's husband, or a Martian with two heads. Whatever form it takes, the wrong face spells trouble.

Of course, maybe you *are* truly in love with this person—but then, maybe you're just getting yourself and the other person into a whole mess of grief. You have to ask yourself: Are the benefits really worth it?

Paula was twenty-eight when she left her husband of seven years. A rising graphic artist in an advertising agency, Paula had a warm but platonic relationship with one of the partners in the agency: a good man in late middle age, himself divorced, who had acted as her professional mentor for several years. This man felt a genuine concern for Paula as she struggled through her first weeks of being on her own again. He took her out for lunch a few times; he listened to her, offering seasoned advice and reassurance. One evening, they went out for dinner and stayed up late drinking wine. One thing led to another, and they ended up in bed together.

The next day, Paula was mortified. The experience had felt uncomfortably like having sex with her father. Worse, she discovered that both her friendship and her professional relations with her mentor suddenly changed, becoming strained and awkward. She'd lost something valuable in her life.

It's hardly surprising that the possibilities for inappropriate liaisons increase greatly after separation. Because you need extra nurturing, you're more open than usual to anyone who comes on strong ("I've always been crazy about you, you know"). But it's also a good idea to be discriminating about how you respond, because your newly single status makes you an irresistible target to some people.

Both women and men can experience emotional or sexual come-ons from colleagues, neighbors, even the husbands or wives of friends or relatives. Sometimes these approaches are easy to resist; sometimes they aren't. Sometimes they're explicit, sometimes they're hidden inside helpful offers of support. And sometimes the offers of support are just that.

My patient Rona certainly saw nothing overtly sexual in the willingness of her best friend's husband, Mel, to come over once in a while to fix a leaky faucet or broken window, now that Rona's husband was gone. Rona and Mel would sit around her kitchen drinking coffee and talking about things. She always found him a caring friend and a good conversationalist, nothing more, whose company she enjoyed on quiet Sunday afternoons. Now and again they'd have long chats on the phone, on the occasions when Rona would call Mel's wife and find she wasn't at home. Once, Mel even took Rona out for lunch on a business day.

The lunch was the last straw for Mel's wife. She wrote Rona a curt, bitter letter telling her that Rona had been seeing far too much of Mel: hers and Rona's friendship was over. Furthermore, she told Mel that if he ever saw Rona again, their marriage was over, too. At one stroke of the pen, Rona had lost two friends.

Of course, the wife's jealous reaction was excessive, and spoke volumes about her own deep insecurities. Yet Rona, although angry and hurt by her friend's suspicions, realized that her need for Mel's friendship had blinded her to the impact it was having on his wife. She resolved to behave more sensitively around couples, who often feel threatened in their own marriages by a friend's separation. And Rona took steps to make friends with single people of both sexes—people with whom she could enjoy less complicated relationships. She joined a women's group and a single parents' organization, thus adding to her circle of friends.

3. SLEEPING AROUND

You could have sex with someone you love, or someone you like, or someone you just want to have fun with. Or you could sleep around. Is there a difference? If so, what is it?

For some recently separated people, sex with different partners—safe sex, of course—is a way to satisfy a powerful drive. But it can also become a way of trying to overcome loneliness, based on the assumption that sleeping with anybody at all is better than sleeping alone. That's a pretty good working definition of sleeping around.

Let me make my moral position on these matters perfectly clear. If you're an adult, and are not involved in a stable, monogamous relationship, you're free to sleep with whomever you wish, provided the other person wants to also: the privilege of two consenting adults.

But this freedom can be taken to the point of self-destructiveness. When it becomes an obsessive quest to avoid sleeping alone in order not to feel lonely, sex becomes something altogether different—an escape, a way of avoiding the feelings that arise from being single. Then, in a sense, you're no longer a consenting adult at all—you're driven, without a choice in the matter.

There's a big distinction between choosing to bed whomever you want and feeling you *have* to sleep with anyone. It's *compulsive* sleeping around that you have to watch out for. If you wake up in the morning and wonder who the hell belongs to that body beside you—Jill or Jane? Jack or Jim?—you may be entering a danger zone. Why? Because you're violating your feelings. You have a valid need to be nurtured, and meeting that need by hopping into bed with anything that moves may briefly make you feel better now and then—but sooner or later, it will involve you with people you'll regret knowing so intimately.

So the message is: Exercise some caution and discrimination. As an adult you can do what you want. Just be careful of your own person—your spirit, if you like. Try not to do yourself any harm.

The odds are that, sooner or later, you'll end up sleeping with someone and wish you hadn't. Well, you won't be the only one: We all have stories we could tell, stories that make us cringe. Let's just hope you can look back on yours some day and laugh about it.

4. WORK AS AVOIDANCE

Sex isn't the only activity people use to escape from their feelings about being separated. Work is another. Staying late at the office, working all weekend, or generally burying yourself in job-related concerns are common stratagems used to avoid the loneliness of going home to an "empty" house or apartment.

As with other kinds of relationships, you need to strike a healthy balance in your relationship to work. In proportion, working can be a constructive activity at this time. It provides a daily framework when other things in your life are collapsing. It creates a sense of structure and stability, like having some ballast in a hurricane.

Throwing yourself vigorously into your work can bring positive spinoffs: more dynamic relationships with colleagues, recognition from superiors, a promotion, more money, or simply the gratification of a job well done. When you're hurting, you need reinforcement of your worth, and if work and career can supply it, that's great.

Of course, it can be very tempting to stay at the office merely because you no longer have to go home at a certain time every night; work expands to fill a vacuum. The larger question is whether your working is becoming excessive. For some of us, work becomes like a drug. Are we letting it rob us of other rewards or gratifications that would contribute to a well-rounded personality and a more balanced, satisfying life?

Work can rob you of leisure time—of the necessary pleasures of relaxing at the ball game, at the theater, in the garden, or just curling up in your living room with a good book, TV show, or video. Work can rob you of exercise and fresh air, which refresh the mind and spirit as well as the body. And work can certainly rob you of friendships and social activities.

Sometimes it seems a whole lot easier to bury yourself in work out of fear of being with others. As a result, you can cut yourself off from the chance to establish new friendships or pursue existing ones, which could provide you with the warm human contact you once enjoyed in your marriage. This makes it harder to put the dead relationship behind you, to get on with building a new life.

Working becomes a pitfall only when it's taken to excess and becomes an excuse to avoid living. Take the case of Ken, an accountant in a big firm. After his separation, Ken increased his workload to a hundred hours a week. His extra effort was noticed, he was promoted, and he made mountains of money. He became president of a professional organization of accountants, and he signed a contract with a publisher to write a textbook. Professionally, he was enormously successful; personally, he was very unhappy.

When Ken came to see me, he'd already been through three different psychiatrists. He wanted help with a sleep disorder, and also with difficulties he was experiencing in his involvements with two different women. Both women were dissatisfied with Ken's lack of emotional commitment and were threatening to cut off the relationship.

It became obvious that Ken's sleep problems and romantic problems had the same source: He was avoiding his feelings through obsessive work. When he tried to sleep, the pain and loneliness he'd been anesthetizing with work came flooding in and kept him tossing and turning. This pattern of emotional avoidance was also sabotaging his relationships with his two women friends.

Ken was so repressed emotionally that his life had become dangerously overbalanced. In the next chapter, we'll see that there are two primary needs in adult life; by working so many hours and hiding from his feelings, Ken was addressing only one of those basic needs. In work, as in all these other potential pitfalls, balance is everything.

5. DISPLACEMENT OF ANGER

We saw in the last chapter that you're inevitably going to feel angry in the aftermath of separation. Anger is part of mourning your dead relationship. You've lost a part of your life in which you've invested heavily, and it's natural to feel angry about that, just as it's natural to feel hurt, sadness, regret, and a host of other powerful and even contradictory emotions.

Feeling angry isn't a pitfall. But what you have to watch out for is becoming *engulfed* by your anger, letting it spill over into other areas of your life—and especially into other relationships, such as with relatives, friends, lovers, or colleagues at work.

Anger, displaced and misdirected from its true source—your dead relationship—can mushroom into a general mistrust of others. Suddenly you find yourself feeling bitter toward the people around you, and what's more, acting the feeling out. In a society that sometimes seems made for couples, you may be resentful of a friend because he or she still has a partner. "It's easy for you," you blurt out, hardly believing you could be saying this. "You've got a husband!"

The danger in taking these kinds of feelings too far is that by displacing your angry, jealous, or hostile feelings onto people around you, you risk cutting yourself off from others, putting unnecessary barriers between you and them by "blaming" them for your emotional distress.

Maureen was forty-nine and bitter after her divorce—with reason. Her husband had taken off with a younger woman while Maureen was in the hospital undergoing a hysterectomy. The divorce battle that ensued was protracted and nasty, focusing on money and the house (the two children were grown up), and on Maureen's attempt to obtain legal rights to some of her husband's pension benefits. Because of his stiff resistance, the battle was costing her a small fortune in legal fees, and she was livid over it.

Ordinarily, Maureen was a fun-loving person who loved to dance. I encouraged her to go out and have a good time at parties and other social events. She went one night to a singles' dance at a neighborhood community center, where, during the course of the evening, several men asked her to dance. The problem was, she was still so angry at her ex-husband that she acted chippy and hostile towards her dancing partners. She concluded that each of them was "after only one thing," and behaved so snappishly that she drove them away.

Maureen was only hurting herself. She had to learn that while her anger was valid, she was letting it interfere with forming new relationships and with simply having fun—which she genuinely wanted to do. Until she learned to restrict her anger to the man who'd caused it, he was still exercising power over her.

Similarly, my patient Peter, a thirty-five-year-old public servant, decided to shun the office Christmas party because the party announcements had declared, "Bring your spouse or Significant Other." Peter agonized over going, but decided against it: "Everyone else will be there in couples," he complained bitterly. "It just bugs the hell out of me."

It was too bad Peter didn't go; he needed to rebuild his social life at the time. He discovered later that not many spouses or Significant Others had shown up at the party after all. Most of his colleagues had been there on their own, just as he would have been. Peter's anger at his single state, and his resulting mistrust of social situations, had led him to exaggerate the problem to his own detriment.

So, when you're feeling angry, suspicious, cynical about the entire opposite sex, try and remember what you're really angry about. Not all men "want only one thing"; not all women are "two-timing sleazy money-grubbing bitches." At the same time, it's inevitable that you'll become inappropriately angry at people sometimes, just as you may go to bed with someone inappropriate. Try to be aware of your anger, and don't let it swallow you up.

6. SHUTTING OUT THE WORLD

Another common but self-defeating response to the emotional pain of separation is cutting yourself off from others. Withdrawing from human contact into a state of isolation can be just as destructive as any of these other pitfalls.

My friend Tom, a forty-one-year-old research chemist, deals with his feelings by saying, "I just don't want to be a burden to anyone." Tom and I used to get together for lunch about once a month; in addition, he and his ex-wife used to see me and my wife socially. Now Tom never calls me—it's always I who call him. As a result, we see each other about half as often as we used to. It makes absolutely no sense for Tom to act this way. Right now, when he's hurting, he needs friendship more than ever.

"Drop over some evening," I tell him. "We'll play computer games or go for a walk or something. Or just sit around and talk."

"Oh no," Tom replies, "you and Judy are busy with your own lives. You have plenty enough to do without having to hear my troubles."

I try to reassure Tom that he's not a burden at all. His real problem is that he feels so bad about himself that he doesn't want to expose his hurt to others. Like a wounded animal, he slinks off into a quiet corner to be alone. "I can handle this on my own," he tells himself. "I don't need anybody else." But that way, the healing process will take a whole lot longer.

As we saw in the previous chapter, there are ways of getting the companionship and sympathy you need without becoming a burden to anyone. Make a list of your friends, relatives, acquaintances. If you see just one or two of them every week, you won't spend so much time with any one person that they'll feel overburdened.

Another common motive for withdrawing from the world is embarrassment or shame over being separated. This can lead people to shun others, even to hide from anything resembling a personal conversation, for fear that the separation will be discovered.

Maureen, the patient I described earlier who loves to dance, suffered from a sense of shame, compounded by her ex-husband's claim that she was inadequate in bed. Maureen had difficulty in shrugging off the painful suspicion that her husband had left her because of her "failures" as a sexual being; she didn't succeed in "keeping her man."

As a result, Maureen hated admitting she was separated. She went to great lengths not only to avoid the subject, but to avoid people altogether, so the subject couldn't come up. When a neighbor—who knew her from the days before her husband had left her for another woman—approached her in a cafeteria and tried to make friendly conversation, Maureen pretended she didn't recognize him.

Gradually, Maureen came around to recognizing that she really had nothing to be ashamed of. Her marriage might have failed, but *she* wasn't a failure. People get separated and divorced all the time nowadays. And besides, was her ex-husband all that wonderful? Was she worse off to be rid of him? Of course not.

Maureen was fond of one of my maxims: "Things could be worse, you know—you could still be married to the jerk." She said she often recalled it when she needed to feel better.

Here's another line worth remembering: "You may be on your own, but you don't need to be alone."

7. TRUE TO YOU IN MY FASHION

You'd be surprised how often separated or divorced people carry on as if they were still married. Some people constantly refer to their ex-spouses in conversation: "George says this," or "Mary thinks I'm that"—it's as if their validity depends on the pretense of continuing the relationship.

Their motive for acting this way is fear of change and the unknown. They're attempting to protect themselves with an illusion of stability and permanence. Being "true" to the dead relationship may lend a comfortable sense of the familiar, but it interferes with actually learning how to function as a newly autonomous adult and enjoying the benefits of independence.

Some people carry on the pretense far beyond the point of reason. A former patient, a woman in late middle age, had been divorced from her husband for ten years; he'd long since remarried, while she lived in her large, echoing, "empty nest" in the suburbs. All the while she remained "Mrs. Brown," drawing her identity from that long-broken connection.

She talked about Mr. Brown as though he were still around. In fact, the two of them had almost no contact, except on family occasions such as weddings and funerals. It struck everyone around her as bizarre. Yet it gave Mrs. Brown the false sense of security that things hadn't really changed after all.

The key issue here is accepting the fact that being on your own *is* very different from being married. For years, you've accommodated another person in your life, but it's no longer necessary to do so. If you had a roommate who moved out of the apartment you both shared, you wouldn't go on leaving half the food in the refrigerator untouched or staying out of the second bedroom—that would seem silly. It is the same with losing a spouse.

Expect your life as a separated person to feel different from your life as a married person. Don't worry that something's "wrong"—it's just different. And try not to let that difference hold you back. You're just as valid and interesting a person as you were before—probably even more so, now that you're differentiating yourself from your couple relationship.

I had a patient, Leslie, who felt reluctant to accept social invitations because she was no longer married. The irony was that Leslie's ex-husband was in the military and often had been away from home for months at a time; then, Leslie hadn't hesitated to accept invitations, simply explaining that Jake was away on duty and she had to attend alone. When Jake returned from his tours of duty, Leslie's social life continued much the same as before. Yet after her separation, she felt she couldn't go out alone! It just didn't feel "right" to her, since being single again was such an unfamiliar sensation. I had to point out to Leslie this blatant contradiction before she began changing her approach to social life.

If you find yourself declining chances to see people socially, just remember the occasion when you once went to a dinner party alone because your spouse was sick or away on business, and you had a lovely time. As a person separate from your relationship, you become more yourself. But if you go on keeping the dead relationship alive in your head, you'll miss the liberating experience of realizing that people appreciate you for yourself, and not as a mere appendage of your ex.

8. WELCOME HOME, CHILD

Another temptation at this time—less common than the others, but definitely a pitfall for some—is to move back in with Mom and/or Dad. Once again, the attraction is the idea of recreating a sense of family and security, of getting nurtured and taken care of. This may work for you briefly as an interim measure, but perpetuated for too long, the remedy becomes worse than the problem; by restoring you to your former status as a child, it undermines your chances for creating a new adult life for yourself.

Gail had been married to a dentist and had an eight-year-old daughter. They'd moved around a lot in their marriage. After separating, Gail didn't want to remain in the city where she'd spent the past two years; yet neither did she feel particularly at home in other cities in which she'd lived. The exception was the community where she'd grown up, and where her parents still lived. So she returned to her hometown in order to have a base to work from in rebuilding her life.

Gail made one crucial decision, however. She resisted the pressure from her mother and father to move back into their big, comfortable home, the very house where she'd grown up. It took a lot of strength, because Gail's daughter wanted to live with Grandma and Grandpa, who weren't above tempting their grandchild with promises of how much fun it would be. It would have been easier for Gail to give in, too; living with her parents would have saved her a lot of trouble and money, by providing built-in babysitting at no charge while she reestablished herself in the work force.

Instead, Gail rented a nice little house, one neighborhood away from her parents. With this arrangement, she could still avail herself of their offers of support for her daughter; when the little girl was sick or had a school holiday, the grandparents could be there to help out. But they couldn't undermine Gail's parental authority by constantly indulging the child, as they would have done if they all lived in the same household.

Also, the arrangements didn't interfere with Gail's independence. She felt more capable, because she managed her own living space, finances, and time. She felt freer to have a social life, to invite colleagues or friends (including men) over for dinner.

As the years passed, Gail felt confirmed in the wisdom of her decision to live alone. She rose to a good executive sales job with the telephone company. Her daughter was doing fine, both academically and socially. Gail had a good relationship going with a man. She felt strong and secure. And when her parents grew frail and needed some care themselves, Gail was close enough that she could help them out, but not so close that her existence was swallowed up by being a nurse to her aged parents.

Gail had struck the right balance in her life.

9. GETTING WASTED

Abusing alcohol and drugs—prescription or otherwise—is common both during and after separation. Many of us are especially vulnerable to substance abuse at this time.

Getting "wasted" is intended to ease the pain. Ultimately, however, it just makes a tough time tougher. Alcohol, tranquilizers, recreational drugs, or even food may offer us temporary relief, but when the next morning rolls around, as it inevitably does, we feel robbed of the physical and emotional strength we need to get through the day in one piece.

Again, it's a question of balance. You may find that alcohol in moderate quantities—one or two drinks—helps you relax without nasty side effects. But for some folks, it becomes hard to stop once they start drinking. And right now, in the emotional hurricane let loose by the separation, you're especially at risk.

This is a good time to find other, more constructive methods of relaxation, such as physical exercise in the form of walking, jogging, working out, or recreational sports; gardening; listening to music; reading; yoga; meditation; or whatever turns you on without wiping you out. Think of it as an opportunity to relax in a positive manner.

One of my patients was a recently separated working mom who looked forward to her shot of chilled vodka every night when she got home from work and had to start dinner for the kids. Her life was hectic, yet lonely. Because she wasn't doing much else to find pleasure or relaxation, the two ounces of vodka gradually became half a bottle. She was getting drunk every evening, which began interfering with her ability to cope with her children, her job, and her life in general. As a result, she ended up losing the job and precipitating a crisis in her finances.

When this patient finally brought herself to admit that she had a problem with alcohol, she committed herself not to drink for that one evening—to find out how it felt to go without booze. Instead of taking the bus home from my office, she walked, to get some fresh air and exercise. The next day, she found she felt a whole lot better than usual. Fortunately, she had the motivation and self-discipline to make it stick. A year and a half later, she still doesn't drink, and her life has come together in a very positive way.

For many heavy drinkers, it's much harder to quit than it was for my patient. These people need sustained support to help them stay away from alcohol, and should consider obtaining therapy, or attending their local branch of Alcoholics Anonymous.

You don't have to be a long-term alcoholic to abuse liquor in a time of crisis. But once that happens, drinking can then become a serious, long-term problem for the future.

Similarly, access to tranquilizers and other prescription drugs, including pain relievers, can lead to abuse when people self-medicate a pain whose real origins are emotional, not physical. In times of acute crisis, a minor tranquilizer or prescribed sleeping medication may be appropriate, but these are intended only as short-term remedies. If you find yourself experiencing an ongoing need for them—if, for example, you're suffering constantly from high anxiety or sleeplessness—it's essential to obtain some psychotherapy or counseling. Otherwise, you may develop a serious dependency on the medication. There are far more constructive ways to deal with depression, anxiety, and insomnia than throwing pills at them.

And, I hardly need to add, be sure to avoid mixing such medications with alcohol. The resulting complications can be very serious indeed.

In the end, substance abuse has the same drawback as all the other excesses described in this chapter: It's not only destructive in and of itself, but it substitutes for genuine efforts to deal with the issues of living on your own again.

10. ARE THE KIDS ALL RIGHT?

Excessive anxiety or guilt over your children can also keep you from living your new life.

Greg, an economics professor in his mid-forties, had custody of his teenage son and daughter. So obsessed was he with their well-being that Greg didn't date for five years after his divorce. He became so preoccupied with cooking for the children, helping them with their homework, and checking on their emotional states that he had virtually no social life of his own. He was afraid that something terrible would happen to his kids if he wasn't there to do everything for them. Yet this was not a great experience for the son and daughter: Dad was always hanging around, they complained; he never seemed able to relax.

Finally taking their comments to heart, Greg enrolled in a gourmet cooking course. This got him out of the house one night a week, and the kids breathed a small sigh of relief. At his cooking class, wonder of wonders, Greg met a woman he liked very much. It was only after he started dating her that he discovered just how much of a burden he'd actually been to his children. His daughter, now in college, confided to Greg's girlfriend that the girlfriend's arrival in their lives had finally made family life tolerable again.

This syndrome occurs even more frequently with women, since mothers still receive custody in the majority of cases. Worries over the children often lead women to try to be Supermom—Mom and Dad rolled into one. It's important to remember that no such person exists, and it's better—and more honest and authentic—just to be yourself. Your children will be satisfied with that.

You can be yourself outside the home as well as inside. If you have a social life of your own, independent of your role as mother and homemaker, you'll feel more fulfilled. Your kids will benefit, too. The emotional climate in the home will improve, and the children will be able to emulate your example and become more positive and self-determining in outlook.

Lina was a patient in her early thirties, who suffered every second weekend, when her two young children went to stay with their father. All weekend, Lina missed them terribly; she just couldn't wait for the sound of her ex-husband's car when he brought them home on Sunday night. Then she threw herself into being Supermom for two more weeks, until she had to face her separation anxiety all over again.

It took Lina a long time, but gradually she learned to handle her insecurity over the kids' absences. Now she realizes they're perfectly okay at their father's place—nothing awful is going to happen to them there. And she's learned to take advantage of her free weekends by doing things she enjoys. She goes out on dates, sees friends, even hires a babysitter on weeknights when the kids are home and she wants to go somewhere on her own.

Of course, every concerned parent wants to fulfill his or her responsibilities toward the children. But if we do this to the exclusion of other interests and concerns, and especially if we neglect doing things for ourselves, a backlash of resentment can build up toward the kids. We can become angry that we don't have a life of our own, and unconsciously take the anger out on the children in inappropriate ways—even though the problem isn't their doing at all, but our own.

CAROL'S PITFALLS

As I've said, no one is immune to the reactions described in this chapter. Our friend Carol was no exception. In the first couple of months after Richard left her, Carol hit no fewer than three of these pitfalls.

At first, she tended to withdraw from others—hiding the fact of her separation, and licking her wounds in private. But eventually, she found it felt better to make a conscious effort to communicate with people on a personal level. When colleagues and neighbors learned that she and Richard had split up and that she was now on her own, most of them were genuinely sympathetic, which Carol found comforting.

The people Carol confided in were mainly colleagues at the office where she worked as personnel manager—a fact connected with the second pitfall she fell into: overdoing things at work. This was understandable, since she hadn't made many friends during her marriage. Carol got overinvolved with her job, putting in endless hours of overtime that detracted from opportunities to enlarge her social life. As a result, she stumbled into the first of two inappropriate relationships.

Carol had to travel on business with a personable male colleague. During a long airplane flight, they shared a few drinks and got to know one another; after many years as a monogamous wife, Carol found the process surprisingly enjoyable. Next day, she and her colleague attended a meeting together, and conducted several interviews with prospective employees, working late into the evening; they finished up with dinner and animated conversation at a restaurant. Afterward, in the hotel, they came close to going to bed together—but at the last minute, Carol decided against it. She realized the dangers it represented: First, he was someone she had to work closely with every day; second, he was, apparently, happily married.

Carol knew her decision had been the right one. But that didn't prevent her from getting into a rebound relationship with her "transitional object"—another co-worker, unmarried. She was quite enthralled with him at first. He showered her with flowers, gifts, and attention; he was eager to spend every minute he could with her; he practically smothered her with affection. It was all a wonderful balm for her bruised ego.

Then the downside emerged. At an office party, he flew into a jealous rage when Carol spent "too much time" chatting with another man. Previously very affectionate, he became verbally abusive. Carol quickly discovered a hidden side of her friend's personality that she didn't like at all: an insecure, possessive, dictatorial side. In fact, it was the negative manifestation of his smothering devotion.

Carol realized that this guy was another version of Richard: a man who'd try to prevent her from being herself. He wasn't right for her at all. She proceeded to extract herself from his grasp, although it took a lot of effort and bluntness, since he was so clinging. Nevertheless, a mere two weeks after she ended the relationship, she saw him laying siege to another woman at work using exactly the same methods he'd used on her. That, she knew, was *his* problem, not hers.

In the meantime, Carol received two benefits from this rebound relationship. Her belief in herself as an attractive, desirable woman was bolstered. And she learned to identify her vulnerability to men who were protective of her, yet also possessive and controlling, and to ask herself the questions: "Do I really want that? Do I really need to be looked after?"

BILL'S PITFALLS

Like Carol, Bill fell prey to overwork—it acted as an anesthetic for his hurt over being booted out of the house by Marie. This was to be expected since, as we've seen, Bill was already a workaholic. Although his obsession with his carpet business had been one of Marie's grievances against him, Bill just became more and more involved in running the store, taking more authority onto himself and delegating less and less to his staff.

This pitfall led in turn to another: getting drunk every night in his lonely apartment. When he returned home late from work, having eaten dinner alone in a restaurant, Bill found he was so tense he couldn't sleep. So he'd have "a snort or two"—meaning, I suspected, four or five—of his favorite scotch, with a beer chaser. Bill was self-medicating with alcohol, using it as a tranquilizer to slow himself down and reduce his high anxiety level. He was also using booze to fill up the emptiness that he felt inside.

Bill let his drinking get so far out of hand that even his kids could tell it was a problem. One weekend, he took Lisa and Jordan to the cottage (he'd surrendered ownership of the cottage to Marie, but she graciously let him use it now and then). As soon as they arrived, Bill started on the beer. By the time he opened his second six-pack, he wasn't much good for taking the kids boating or fishing, or for cooking them dinner. "Daddy," said eleven-year-old Lisa matter-of-factly, "you're drinking too much." The next weekend, she showed remarkable insight and maturity when she announced on her arrival at his apartment: "If you have any more than three beers, I'm going home to Mom."

Bill realized his daughter was right. He took her warning to heart and began to cut back his drinking. He also had to learn more constructive ways to slow himself down and to start enjoying life.

Bill's other pitfall was a tendency to continue thinking of himself as still married to Marie. He had difficulty accepting the fact that the marriage, which he'd taken for granted for so many years, was really over—that this wasn't just a bad dream, or some little tantrum of hers. He carried on, playing the roles of the dutiful husband and good father, the provider of money, treats, and transportation.

At first, Marie colluded in the fantasy that, in some sense, they were still together. When Lisa begged Bill to stay over in the house one Friday night, because he was driving her to her ballet competition early the next morning, Bill asked Marie what he should do; Marie said he could sleep on the sofa in the basement rec room. This sort of thing happened several times. One night, Bill slept not in the basement, but upstairs in the former conjugal bed. Although sex for old times' sake didn't result in a reconciliation between him and Marie, it did feed the children's false expectations that their parents would get back together.

All of Bill's pitfalls resulted from a single problem: He wasn't doing anything to be his own person, with needs of his own that required attention.

Stage Two
Exploring

After the first three months or so, life on your own moves into an exploratory stage. Now you can try out new ways of dealing with your needs and relationships. This stage typically lasts until the end of Year One.

Your explorations will be both inward and outward. After grieving over your dead relationship, your introspection becomes more hopeful. It's possible to look backwards with dry eyes and examine what went wrong in your relationship, and why—and also to look ahead and consider where you want to go from here. After all, as Yogi Berra once said, "If you don't know where you're going, you might end up someplace else."

In this stage, we'll look at how you're going to start thinking and behaving differently, in your own best interests. This involves understanding what your adult needs are, and how to meet them successfully. And it involves revising some existing relationships—with your ex-partner and with your children, if any. As you work through this stage, you're putting your dead relationship to rest, and getting ready to make new connections with the world.

Chapter Four

Meeting Your Adult Needs

There are just two basic needs that you have as an adult man or woman in our society: *to be somehow productive, and to be cared about as a person.*

In this chapter, I'll explain how these primary adult needs apply to the separated or divorced person—or, for that matter, to the still-married. I'll show how these adult needs differ from the primary needs of children, in both their nature and in the ground rules for meeting those needs. Finally, I'll show how learning to meet your adult needs, according to adult ground rules, can provide you with the foundation for a rewarding and fulfilling new life as a single person—a foundation you'll need whether or not you eventually remarry.

Three months after her separation from Richard, Carol swept in for her weekly session at my office. Yes, *swept in.* I immediately sat up and took notice. Something was unquestionably different about Carol that day, and it wasn't just her new hairstyle, shorter and more streamlined than usual. (For all I knew, she might have been wearing new shoes or a new dress, too—I'm not very perceptive about that sort of thing.)

No, it was something more fundamental: something about the way she held herself. Instead of pressing her back ramrod-straight against the chair, she leaned forward confidently. She draped one hand casually over her crossed knees, instead of anxiously clutching her purse strap. She didn't automatically pull the Kleenex box on the sidetable a little closer. There was something different about her eyes too: They were animated, dancing. She pressed her lips together as if trying to suppress a grin.

All I needed to say was, "Well?"

"Well!" she replied. "I think you're going to be proud of me."

I sat back and listened. On the previous Saturday, Carol explained, she'd gone and done something she'd wanted to do for a very long time. She'd signed up for membership in a tennis club, paying for three months' worth of lessons, plus an annual membership fee that entitled her to full use of the club's facilities—the freedom, as she significantly put it, to go whenever she pleased.

"Now, I realize," she added, "that it doesn't sound like a very big deal. But for me, it's a huge step."

I knew exactly what she meant. For years during her marriage to Richard, Carol had loved playing tennis, but her ability to enjoy the game had been severely curtailed. She and Richard would play together whenever they traveled on vacation, but he was always so fussy and demanding about her game, pointing out her faults and errors, that it spoiled the fun for her.

For some reason, Richard had never been interested in joining a tennis club at home. Carol suspected that, as in other aspects of their marriage, he'd simply found her to be an unsatisfactory partner. After all, according to him she was a dull conversationalist, a mediocre cook, an inadequate hostess. Why would he want to play tennis with such a klutz?

Of course, before now, Carol could have joined the club herself. But that would have meant taking action independently of Richard, and she hadn't been ready to do such a thing: It might have upset him. She'd always operated on the assumption that she couldn't afford to incur Richard's displeasure. Now that she no longer had Richard around, she didn't have to worry about his disapproval. But there was much more to it than that.

"Doing this was scary," Carol admitted. "I had to go to the club all by myself. I didn't know anyone there, and I didn't have anyone to go with. But—well, I don't have any friends who play tennis, so I realized that if this was ever going to happen, it was up to me.

"And not only that—once I'd signed up, they told me that there's going to be a social evening at the club this Saturday. So I made another scary decision. I said I'd go to the social—on my own!"

In the grand scheme of things, Carol's behavior at the tennis club may seem trivial. But for her, it was a breakthrough. Although only a first step, it was a big one. She'd recognized two of her important needs—to have fun playing a game she enjoyed, and to make new friends in the process—and she had taken the initiative to meet those needs herself.

In fact, Carol had reached a turning point in her recovery from her shattered marriage. Over time, she would reap numerous rewards from her decision: She'd have a good time learning and playing tennis; she'd enjoy the physical exercise; she'd rebuild self-confidence as her game improved; and, not least, she'd meet new people who shared her interests.

But most of all, Carol would discover a vital truth about herself: that she is a capable, competent adult, with the power to meet her own needs. It was something she'd never known with Richard.

THE GROUNDHOG ANALOGY

Anyone recovering from the end of a marriage or a long-term relationship eventually reaches this transition stage, just as Carol did. It's a time of dawning hopes and emerging expectations—exciting, but scary, too.

It's exciting because you're on the verge of embarking on a new life, a fresh stage in your existence. But it's scary because you're not at all certain what this new life holds in store. All you know for sure is that it's going to be very different from your old life.

Typically, you'll arrive at this stage around three or four months after the final break with your ex. (Don't worry if you find yourself getting there later. It's okay not to be typical.) By now, you've already endured, and survived, the worst of the breakup experience: You've suffered through the crisis itself—the sheer agony of having a once-vibrant relationship turn terminally ill and then die. You've endured the mourning period—the black, depressing, frightening time when you felt emotionally destitute, when you could only grieve for what you'd lost, when the best you could hope for was to hang on and survive from day to day. You've also encountered some of the pitfalls I described in Chapter 3—those self-defeating but entirely normal attempts to cope with your turmoil—attempts which just seemed to lead you deeper into discouragement.

All of these stages felt pretty horrible at the time. But now, a few months after separating, you're getting through all that. And, like Puxanatawny Phil, the old groundhog who leaves his burrow to get some concept of how much winter is left and how long it's going to be until spring, you're starting to feel ready to peer out over the edge of your dark, emotional pit. Now it feels like time to take stock of the world, to see what's out there for you. Somehow, life isn't completely black anymore.

This is an important moment. Your grieving done, you have the strength to look back with dry eyes and see what went wrong, and why. You also have the strength to look forward—to begin asking, as Carol did, "What do I want? What do I, as an adult, really need?"

ADULT NEEDS, CHILDHOOD NEEDS

Since human life is a developmental process that passes through various stages, we have to go back first and look at the time when we were tiny tots.

Like adults, infants also have two basic needs—but they're fundamentally different in nature from adult needs. One of our primary childhood needs is *to be taken care of*; the other is *to learn*.

Little children absolutely must have these two needs met. If somebody hadn't taken care of us when we were little children, we would have died. Beyond that, in order to survive and develop psychologically and socially, we needed to learn practically everything—to eat, dress, walk, cross the street, read, and so on.

The ground rules that a child must follow to get these two childhood needs met are quite simple: If you're a good little boy or girl, somebody will take care of you. And if you're a good little boy or girl, somebody will teach you what you need to know in order to survive and develop.

The biggest threat to any little child comes when a parent is angry, and the child becomes afraid: "If Mommy or Daddy is angry, maybe they won't take care of me anymore! If they won't take care of me, I'll die!" So the child falls into line and behaves, maybe asking for a kiss afterwards, just to make sure everything's okay again.

As we grow older and go off to school, some of the responsibility for meeting our childhood needs is transferred to the educational authorities. But the needs are still the same, and so are the ground rules for meeting them: If you're a good little boy or girl, you'll learn what you need at school. And if you're a good little boy or girl, you'll be taken care of at school. Meanwhile, we're still learning and being taken care of at home, too. So, with any luck, life is relatively happy and secure.

At around age ten or twelve, we become increasingly involved with our peers. Family and school still play a role in meeting our two primary needs, but now, so does the peer group. The ground rules are adapted: If you're a good little boy or girl *within the values and mores of the peer group*, we'll all teach each other, and we'll all take care of each other.

In our teens, the biological imperative nudges us into pairing off. However awkwardly at first, we start learning how to make and maintain a one-to-one relationship. The pairing-off process may seem crude and primitive from an adult point of view, but the relationships thus formed soon grow stronger and more intense. And since teenagers still need to be taken care of, even while moving beyond family, school, and peer group, they base their relationships on the proposition: *You take care of me, I'll take care of you.* This is the ground rule most of us carry into our first intimate relationships—and into our marriages.

For our purposes here, I arbitrarily define adolescence as the period from ages fifteen to twenty-five, give or take a couple of years. As those of us past the age of majority are well aware, we don't magically become mature adults at twenty-one. The maturity level of a twenty-three-year-old is vastly different from that of a thirty-year-old. By this definition, a young marriage or partnership is the coupling, psychologically speaking, of two adolescents.

This adolescent basis for relationships continues well into our mid-to-late twenties. Despite our growing independence at that age, we're still learning, and we still require a degree of being taken care of. We tend to transfer that responsibility to our partners, and they to us—which is fine, because love and marriage, along with our work and other interests, help provide the secure foundations for a developing identity. The adolescent ground rule is appropriate to this age and stage of development.

Needless to say, there are many other factors determining compatibility between partners—social background, educational level, mutual interests, sexual attraction, and so on. But whatever the young couple's circumstances, the basis of their marriage pact is:

"We're in this together, so you take care of me, and I'll take care of you."

And they lived happily ever after—right?

Wrong.

THE END OF THE ADOLESCENT MARRIAGE

Adult psychological development doesn't stop with our twenties. As Gail Sheehy showed in *Passages*, we continue developing through various stages all our lives.

So it is, inevitably, with marriage, which, as a relationship between two individuals with changing needs, also must change. Unless it grows into a flexible and dynamic partnership, it becomes stagnant and unbearably confining.

There's just one problem: Men are retarded.

That's my way of saying that, just as six-year-old girls are ahead of six-year-old boys in terms of verbal, social, and academic development, wives tend to be ahead of their husbands in reaching the next stage of adult development. Of course, their husbands do catch up eventually—although sometimes it's too late.

For a woman, the next stage of adult development usually occurs in her early thirties. For a man, it may not occur until his late thirties or even early forties.

This is the stage when we begin to realize, vaguely at first, and then with increasing certainty, that our needs are not being met. The adolescent needs to learn and to be taken care of are no longer enough to motivate and fulfill us. The old basis for life and marriage that saw us through our twenties isn't adequate for our thirties.

For the woman in her early thirties, this recognition registers as a gnawing dissatisfaction. She feels a sense of loss, a void at the center of her life, a conviction that something important is missing. Men, being retarded, haven't twigged to this yet. They carry on in the same old way, operating on the basis of the old needs, the old marriage pact. They can't help it. Meanwhile, women begin to ask themselves questions—big questions their husbands typically haven't asked yet.

A woman thinks to herself, "I spend all my time being a good little girl, taking care of others, and being taken care of. I spend my days being somebody's wife, and somebody's mom, and somebody's cook, maybe somebody's employee as well. But I feel more and more like an object. What's it all about? What's in it for *me?*"

She has an acute sense of nonfulfillment. Merely being very good at playing her role as Mommy/Little Girl doesn't solve her problem. What she must do is identify what her new adult needs are, and why they're not being met. And to do that, it's crucial for her to see what has happened to her in the period between her late twenties and early thirties, while she was being a good wife and homemaker and, perhaps, mother. A lot has happened, even if she hasn't been fully conscious of it.

EVOLVING NEEDS

Essentially, the woman's two primary childhood needs have evolved into her two primary adult needs. And the ground rules for getting those needs met have changed too.

The need to learn has evolved into the need *to be somehow productive.*

Meeting this adult need doesn't depend on being a good little girl or good little boy any longer. It depends on going out and doing things for ourselves, for our own good reasons, according to our own objectives, standards, and values. It depends on doing things that give us a deep sense of satisfaction as mature adults, yielding a conviction of time and effort well spent.

How we personally define productivity varies enormously from person to person. There is no "correct" set of goals and activities to which to devote ourselves. For example, one woman may choose to branch out from her roles as mother and homemaker to take a job that provides her with the stimulation and reward she's been missing. Meanwhile, another woman may go in exactly the opposite direction, feeling her need to be productive satisfied by leaving the work force to bear a child. Yet another woman may fulfill this need through volunteer community work, hobbies, artistic expression, or further education.

The key point is that we're no longer doing things to please others. The satisfaction that comes from being productive comes from you and goes to you.

Here's an illustration I always use with my patients to demonstrate the distinctive nature of adult motivation. As an adult, you have a workspace that's important to you, whether at the office, the store, or at home—perhaps it's a workshop or sewing room or den. From time to time, you look at this workspace and decide to clean it up. After you've thrown out some things and organized and tidied up the rest, and everything is in its proper place, you feel good about the job you did. Nobody else needs to know what you've done—you did it by yourself, for yourself, because *you* wanted to, and it feels good.

If you tell a fifteen-year-old, "Go clean up your room, you'll feel good about it," he or she will look at you as if you're crazy. The fifteen-year-old *won't* feel good about it—but the fifteen-year-old *will* clean up the room if the punishment for not doing so is losing an allowance or being grounded. He or she will do it under duress, to be a good little boy or good little girl—but not for any intrinsic reward. It's a crucial distinction.

In parallel to the evolving need to be somehow productive, the old need to be taken care of has also evolved—into the adult need to *be cared about as a person.*

This, too, is a seismic change. And it's accompanied by a similar change in the ground rules for meeting the need. Being cared about as a person has nothing to do with playing roles and being a good little girl or boy. It has to do first and foremost with yourself: You care about yourself as a person, you answer to yourself as a person, and you get cared about as that person.

To see what this momentous change means for a marriage, think about friendship. At one time or another, most of us have had one or more close friends. They're the people with whom you can be yourself. When you're together with a friend, you don't have to play the role of good little boy or good little girl—you can just *be.*

In a friendship, there's no requirement that you should have to be taken care of, either. Of course your friends care *about* you—if you're in some trouble, if your house burns down, they'll rally around and help you in your hour of need. That's understood. But your friends assume that normally you can take care of yourself, like any capable, competent adult, and you assume the same about them.

Our relationships with friends are marked by mutual respect, mutual trust, mutual caring *about*. Friends don't try to change you; you don't try to change them. They like and accept you as you are, with all your flaws and imperfections, and you like and accept friends the same way—they're allowed to have flaws. You say to yourself, "That's just the way he or she is."

This model of friendship can equally apply to adult marriage. A good adult marriage contains those same basic qualities of mutual respect, trust, and caring *about*. But those qualities are difficult to achieve when grown men and women run around playing roles, being good little boys and girls, and taking care of each other's lives—as you probably did in your marriage.

The dissatisfied woman in her early thirties who feels like an object, restlessly seeking new meaning in her life, has already run into this dilemma. Some women, like my former patient Janet, tie themselves in knots trying to be Supermom and Superwife, and then get angry and overwhelmed by it all. In Janet's case, her marriage had outlived whatever value it once held for her. Yet she believed she was indispensable to her husband, who could scarcely boil water. Even when she received an invitation to visit her sister in another city for two weeks, she felt guilty and reluctant about going because she was convinced her husband and daughter couldn't manage without her.

In the end, Janet went to her sister's anyway—and discovered on returning home that her husband and daughter had managed just fine. They'd not only survived, but they showed Janet that they had a good relationship between them. This gave her the encouragement she needed to stop playing her caretaker role and leave a marriage that would never be right for her.

Another woman might respond by trying to become an even better little girl, trying even harder to be Superwife and Supermom—in addition, frequently, to holding down a demanding job. And when she finds that this still doesn't meet her needs, she may get angry and become a *bad* little girl—"disobeying," breaking the "rules" of her marriage by refusing to cook, or to be faithful, and so on.

But her needs still won't be met—because she still hasn't recognized how they've changed. The fact is, she's addressing the wrong needs. Whether she's in a married relationship or not, she still has to learn what her adult needs are, and that meeting them doesn't depend on the approval or disapproval of her partner—it depends only on herself.

What about the male of the species? Like the turtle in Aesop's fable, he slowly but steadily catches on and catches up. He won't necessarily win the race—actually, there is no race—but just as surely as the female, he eventually recognizes that there's something missing in his life.

By his late thirties or early forties, the male may realize he's been running himself ragged being a terrific provider, caretaker, and father all these years, but there's something wrong: It doesn't work for him anymore. Expecting in turn to be taken care of by his wife, he's been a Daddy/Little Boy, a grown-up version of his childhood self. Finally, playing those roles just isn't enough any longer.

(If he has a flair for black humor, he may even decide there *is* one way he could become the perfect caretaker/provider: *drop dead*. That way, he'd provide the wife and kids with all the financial security of a nice, rich insurance windfall; the mortgage would be paid off; his wife might even receive a widow's pension if he played his cards right. Alive, he could never take such good care of her. But, somehow, this doesn't seem like a fair deal.)

So, to address his growing malaise, a man has to go through the same process a woman does: learning to meet his adult needs to be productive in his own right, and to be cared about as a person.

BILL'S STORY

In earlier chapters, we met my patient Bill and saw how much blood, sweat, and tears he'd poured into his retail carpet business. After buying out his brothers, Bill took on an even bigger work load in the store. His increased control over the business enabled him to cut costs, boost sales, and take home bigger profits, but at the price of a punishing seventy-hour work week.

Bill's wife, Marie, liked the life-style made possible by his success, but deeply resented the evenings and weekends he took away from their life together. And yet, ironically, Bill told himself he was doing it all for his family. Even after his separation, he still clung to the idea that he was "a good provider"—it was a major part of his identity.

It was essential for Bill to understand that being excessively wrapped up in the breadwinner/provider role had not only undermined his former marriage, but had unbalanced his whole life, jeopardizing his chances for *future* happiness. He had to start seeing to his other needs as well, which he was neglecting at his peril.

One day, Bill arrived for his session with an oddly bemused look on his face. It was a full four months since he'd moved, at Marie's insistence, out of the matrimonial home he'd slaved so hard to pay for.

"You'll never guess how I spent last weekend," he said slyly.

"You're right," I said, suspecting some salacious tale of bachelor debauchery. "But let me try. You had an orgy right there in the carpet store."

"Hell no!" Bill replied indignantly. (He is a serious man, and he seldom found my banter amusing.) "I spent it with the kids."

"The kids?" I acted dumbfounded. "A whole weekend?"

This was a first. As Bill described it, he'd always spent Friday evenings in the store, because it was such a busy time. But last Friday, Marie had asked him to take the kids after school instead of waiting until Saturday morning. Eager to see them, he'd agreed, and for once had left the store at five o'clock, entrusting it to the hands of his manager.

He picked up the kids and brought them to his place. He ordered in from their favorite pizza joint, then they all spent a quiet but fun evening together, sitting around playing Clue. Lisa was Miss Scarlet, Jordan was Professor Plum, Bill was Colonel Mustard, and Mrs. Peacock committed murder in the conservatory with the candlestick. Next day, Bill drove Lisa to her ballet class and Jordan to his Little League practice. He managed to restrict himself to a forty-five-minute visit to the store—just to make sure everything was going okay and there were no problems that required his attention. He came away with new admiration for his staff's competence. Was it possible they could actually manage without him?

Later, he went to a video store with the kids and rented a couple of movies—one of Lisa's choosing and one of Jordan's. Bill made a huge batch of popcorn at home, which they ate on Saturday evening while watching the videos together. On Sunday, he revived his modest and long-neglected talents as a cook, whipping up buttermilk pancakes for breakfast and chili for lunch. When the hour came to deliver Lisa and Jordan to their mother, he scarcely knew where the time had gone. He realized he hadn't thought about the carpet store for a full twenty-four hours.

"It was the quietest weekend I've spent in fifteen years," Bill told me with an air of wonderment. "But you know, it was a lot of fun. And I felt good about it."

The underlying reason why Bill felt so good was that he was starting to be his own person. He was starting to recognize that he had needs of his own—for the companionship of his kids outside of tasks and obligations, for quiet family pleasures—needs that his breadwinner/provider role couldn't meet.

In the process of learning how to meet those needs, Bill was discovering how to care about himself as a person. And that's the crucial first step toward getting cared about by others.

IT'S UP TO YOU

Now we're getting to the bottom line of all this. Here you are, a few weeks or months after the end of your relationship, looking back on what went wrong. Perhaps you can see it now: Beneath the unique circumstances of your breakup, beneath the grievances, disputes, and recriminations, the harsh words and hurtful acts, the underlying problem was that your real, adult needs were not being met in the relationship.

You still have those needs. You still need to be productive somehow. And you still need to be cared about as a person. Like Carol and Bill, you have to find ways to meet those needs in your newly single state, because if you don't, you're going to continue feeling unfulfilled and unhappy—and that just isn't necessary!

Now is the time to start finding your own path to meeting your adult needs. It was impossible even to think about this during your grieving process. You were so angry then, so sad, so frightened, so overwhelmed, that the whole concept of "adult needs" would have seemed academic, pointless, and irrelevant. Your overriding need then was simply to survive, to pull through. You were like someone in a war zone: The bombs were exploding everywhere, and you just had to find shelter.

Now you can afford to ponder how you want to be productive, and how you can be cared about as a person. Only you can do the work of finding the answers for yourself, the ones that are right for your particular case. I can show you where to look for those answers. In later chapters, we'll consider your wide range of options and opportunities for meeting your adult needs in a way that's appropriate and fulfilling for you.

In the meantime, here are a few guidelines:

• *Being a person in your own right isn't as hard as it looks.*

As we saw in Chapter 3, it's normal after your marriage breakdown to think, "I can't handle this on my own. I've got to find somebody else." But if you immediately go looking for a new partner to fulfill your needs for you, you'll ultimately be disappointed. In order to be productive and cared about as a person, you have to *be* a person first—someone who can meet his or her own needs, not an object looking for a caretaker.

It really isn't all that difficult. In fact, you're already doing a fine job of being a person when you're with your friends. You and your friends enjoy each other's company because you can relax and be yourself. Your friends don't think you're wimpy, or fragile, or helpless. They don't feel they have to protect you, take care of you, change you, control you—they like and accept you as you are.

That's what being a person means. It's already happened in your life: Friends like and accept you. So will the rest of the world. So will you.

• *You answer only to yourself.*

When you were busy being a Daddy/Little Boy or Mommy/Little Girl, you weren't really answering to yourself the way an adult does. You were being responsible to your partner/caretaker—that other Daddy/Little Boy or Mommy/Little Girl who, in turn, was being responsible to you.

That's all over now. As a single person, you are responsible *for* yourself. And you're responsible *to* yourself to be the best person you can be. This will remain true even if you enter a new love relationship—and even if you remarry. Once you've taken full responsibility to and for yourself, with all the self-determination that entails, there's no reason to ever return to the old adolescent way of doing things.

• *No adult can ever adequately look after another adult.*

Whenever you notice yourself slipping back into the old you-take-care-of-me, I'll-take-care-of-you syndrome, whenever you even feel tempted, consider for a moment the price to be paid.

To illustrate: If you as an adult really want to get taken care of adequately, there's only one place to go—a hospital. There, you'll be taken care of *really* well. You'll be clothed, bathed, fed, and so completely regulated that you won't have to make any decisions for yourself whatsoever. You'll be told when to eat, sleep, exercise, and go to the bathroom. And if you're a very good little patient, you'll be praised and pampered and told you'll get well.

The only catch is the price you have to pay to get taken care of so completely: You have to sign away all your rights as a person. This also happens when you try to get another adult to take care of you.

But the truth is, no adult can ever adequately take care of another adult. What happens when they try? They don't do it right. It isn't humanly possible. So the one being cared for becomes hurt, angry, and resentful: "If you loved me, you'd take better care of me. I've signed away my rights to you and you're still not looking after me perfectly!"

The caretaker, who's in an impossible position, feels the same way: "I'm trying my damnedest to take care of you, and you're still not happy. You make me angry!"

Everybody ends up angry, all of the time. It's a lose-lose situation.
• *Dependence means being controlled.*

Do you really want your existence controlled by another person? That, too, is part of the price for being cared for.

A former patient of mine, whom I'll call Vivian, had made a bad deal by signing away her rights to her Daddy/Little Boy husband. His was an extreme case of controlling behavior. He had to have his dinner on the table by six o'clock every evening and wouldn't "let" Vivian leave home to work. Her job was to stay home, look after the kids and her husband, and be controlled by him. At one point, he installed an intercom system throughout the house, with two-way speakers in every room. He was able to set the system so that, sitting at the central-command console, he could keep track of Vivian's movements from room to room. This made it ever so easy to issue orders to her; she was never out of the sound of his voice, never beyond his control.

Vivian isn't married to her husband anymore. This is not a cause of great sadness to her. He still tries to control her—by sending her "round-trip memos" about the care of the children, to which she's supposed to reply on the bottom half of the memo form. She ignores them.

Vivian's husband was a domestic tyrant. But rather than coming from personal strength, his controlling behavior reflected his

weaknesses; he, too, wanted to be taken care of. Vivian had bought into a mutual dependency pact—as a lot of us do.
• *You can be un-dependent.*
    Your antidote to the catch-22 of dependency is to become un-dependent.

Being un-dependent means answering to yourself for your decisions and actions—being, as I put it earlier, responsible to and for yourself.

It's a little different from being *in*dependent, if you construe independence as meaning *total* self-sufficiency, being unattached and unconnected to others, which has a lonely feel to it. Un-dependent is something you can be while still sharing your life with others—a friend, a lover or, yes, a spouse.

A kind of litmus test for measuring your un-dependency quotient is how you feel about the following situation: Let's say you have a housemate, with whom you share an understanding that you eat dinner together every Wednesday. This Wednesday, something comes up at work, forcing you to be ninety minutes late. Do you phone your housemate to say you're going to be late? Sure you do—it's only considerate.

Suppose, instead, you have a spouse with whom you expect to have dinner tonight, but that same obligation comes up at the office. How do you feel about phoning your spouse to say you're going to be late? Do you feel resentful having to "check in," having to report to "Mom" or "Dad"? Or do you feel it's perfectly reasonable to call, out of respect and consideration, since your spouse's time is just as valuable as yours?

If you're in an I'll-take-care-of-you you-take-care-of-me relationship, you'll feel resentful having to be a good little boy or good little girl. If you're un-dependent, you'll feel fine about calling. Your approach to the relationship makes a world of difference.

IT'S POSSIBLE TO CHANGE

Becoming an un-dependent person, responsible to and for yourself, is necessary for the sake of your happiness. This is true no matter what your marital situation, but it's especially necessary when you're separated or divorced.

Some people may have trouble accepting this change in you. It may inconvenience them, because they have a vested interest in keeping you dependent, either as their caretaker or the one who gets cared for. Or, like many people, they simply may be inflexible, slow to adapt to change in others. Either way, you can't let them stop you.

Sometimes, we have conflicts with people close to us when we make a change of this magnitude. When Vivian began asserting her right to pursue interests of her own, her husband's controlling behavior became even more rigid. One evening, he arrived home expecting his hot dinner to be on the table at six o'clock as usual. But, as Vivian had explained to him that morning, she had a church choir practice and had to leave right away. She'd prepared his dinner and left it in the oven; all he had to do was serve it to himself.

When Vivian arrived home after choir practice, she found her husband still waiting to be served his dinner, which had remained in the oven, drying up. His insistence on maintaining their respective roles was even more powerful than his insistence on eating his dinner at the same time every night.

Faced with this childish yet tyrannical behavior, designed to keep her as a dependent Mommy/Little Girl with no rights of her own, Vivian wisely ended her marriage; it finally became clear to her that her husband refused to change. But she could change, and she did. At the same time, she realized she couldn't blame her husband entirely for the shortcomings of their marriage. For years, she'd given away her rights to personhood in order to be taken care of. But if she was ever going to be cared about as a person, she had to *be* a person, by exercising those rights. And when her husband couldn't handle that, she knew she didn't need the marriage any longer.

It's natural to worry what will happen when we change—to wonder whether those around us will respond positively or negatively. But most people aren't as absurdly hidebound as Vivian's husband. When you make changes to meet your own needs, most of the people close to you will learn to adapt and deal with you differently.

My patient Gloria learned this when she refused to deny her legitimate needs for the sake of her husband, Gil. In her early thirties, Gloria was a classic case: A mother of three, she knew beyond a doubt that she needed to do something interesting outside the home. Gil said he'd "allow" her to have a job, but she had to be home when the kids returned from school. Gloria replied that she didn't want a job just yet; she wasn't ready. She'd prefer to take a creative writing course being offered two nights a week at the local college. Gil refused to "allow" this, on the grounds they couldn't afford it. For the same reason, he wouldn't agree to buy the sewing machine Gloria wanted. Meanwhile, he spent money on a new lawn mower, because he felt the old one wasn't working properly. The family spending priorities were Gil's priorities.

Gloria started providing day-care services to two preschool children in the neighborhood. After three months, she'd earned enough to buy the sewing machine and enroll in the evening course. She did both, without so much as asking Gil's permission. When he saw the sewing machine and confronted her, she replied simply, "I bought it with my own money. I'm taking that course, too, starting in January."

Interestingly enough, Gil came around very quickly. He made sure he was home in time to be with the kids on Gloria's course nights, and began accepting her other initiatives more easily. Gil found he could deal with the reality of Gloria's increased independence after all; it had been the *idea* of losing power in the relationship that had threatened him.

AN UN-DEPENDENT YOU

If people truly care about you as a person, sooner or later they'll be willing to support your efforts to meet your needs. They'll accept and embrace the new you, happy to see you taking steps to be the person you want to be.

Nonetheless, it's always up to you to make the first moves. The you-take-care-of-me and I'll-take-care-of-you trap is a game requiring two players. Once you stop playing the game, and begin functioning as your own person, the ground rules change.

Not only spouses play the game; even friends may be resistant to your changing. If they're real friends, they'll eventually respond as real friends do. But if they don't respond in kind, you may find you don't need their "friendship" anymore. In the end, you'll keep around you only those who can deal with you as a capable, competent, un-dependent adult.

As you become increasingly willing to go ahead and meet your own needs, you'll discover the tremendous excitement of opening up new horizons, realizing new possibilities. You'll be free to be yourself. Carol and Bill both discovered that freedom. Later on, we'll see how they used it. But at this stage, they learned how rewarding it feels to live in an un-dependent way. Carol was excited and energized by the realization that she could fulfill her long-suppressed desire to join the tennis club. Bill was deeply gratified to find he could take time away from his business to be with his kids without feeling guilty. From that point on, they felt the future was theirs—the world and its bounty out there for the picking.

You can feel the same.

Chapter Five

Dealing With Your Ex: "I'll Never Understand Women," or, "Men Are Such Bastards"

W hen a couple splits up, the partners may fantasize about never having to see each other again. What a relief! What liberty! What bliss!

In reality, however, most separated people continue to have some sort of relationship with each other, at least for a while. The old relationship is, of course, dead; but there's usually some form of continuing contact, and how you handle it can make a big difference to your happiness.

This is especially true if children are involved. In that event, a separated couple will have to work out new ways of cooperating over such matters as visiting rights or joint-custody arrangements, child support, in-laws, who drives the kids to camp, or who spends vacations with them. Child-raising issues can keep ex-spouses involved with each other for many years—although their relationship has drastically changed from its former state.

Even if there are no children involved, and little need for continuing contact in the long run, it may still be necessary to communicate on matters of mutual concern. And this may happen at just the time when it's most difficult and painful to do so. During the acute phase of breaking up, when all you want to do is forget about your ex-partner and the dead relationship, it seems you can't avoid discussing who gets the sound system, the cat or the jacaranda plant.

For some people, such as the divorcing couple in the novel and movie *The Accidental Tourist*, these matters can be settled with a bare minimum of discussion; for others, communicating through lawyers is preferable. Usually there's some practical matter, or some piece of unfinished emotional business, that needs to be worked out—and that can be hard to handle, given the sadness, grief, and anger you're feeling as you mourn your dead relationship.

Is there a way to make communication any easier at this time?

There is. Basically, you have to learn to recognize where your ex-partner is coming from psychologically when he or she says those things that upset or irritate you, or just plain drive you up the wall. Realizing what your ex is going through may not necessarily change your feelings toward him or her, but it will help you understand the fears that drive his or her actions. And that, in turn, will help you deal constructively with any negative, anxiety-provoking behavior that might be inflicted on you.

That's what this chapter is all about—helping you to negotiate a new and more constructive way of dealing with your ex, thus freeing you to get on with your own life and enabling you to become a capable, competent adult, on your own again.

GEORGE AND MARY ELLEN

You've seen how much of Chapters 1 through 4 applies to you; a lot of it applies to your ex also. Although some of your ex's specific behaviors may occasionally seem weird from your perspective (certainly less reasonable than your own!), you can generally assume that he or she is going through the same psychological processes you are—the same stages described in this book.

Even if your ex-partner appears to be doing just fine, thank you—he's moved in with that little tramp of a secretary, or she's staying in your nice comfortable home, while you're living in a dismal bachelor flat and forking out big bucks—in reality, he/she also inhabits an emotional pressure cooker right now, which will influence his or her behavior toward you.

Sometimes, it's tempting to say: "I don't care what he/she is going through!" That's fine—you don't have to care. Maybe you're even glad your ex is hurting—and that's fine, too. But your ex will be easier to deal with if you take the trouble to understand the emotional basis underlying his/her actions.

For some, it can be equally tempting to take the opposite approach, to say, "Poor thing, he/she is in such distress, I wish I could make it better." So you tell yourself you have some responsibility to come to your ex's rescue—to help set up the new apartment, hang the curtains, winterize the car, or whatever. But that isn't your job. Getting all wrapped up in your ex's problems isn't useful to you right now.

This point is illustrated by my patient Mary Ellen and her husband, George. Both in their mid-fifties, they'd been married twenty-nine years when George told Mary Ellen he was gay. Although he hadn't accepted his homosexuality initially, relationships he'd had with several men in recent years persuaded him that it was his true sexual orientation. For the sake of honesty, he'd decided it was time to tell Mary Ellen and end the marriage, now that their two grown children had moved away.

Mary Ellen was devastated. Profoundly hurt and deeply confused, she began to question the meaning and value of each of those twenty-nine years—"the best years of my life," as she kept calling them. She'd thought she had a stable marriage, whereas it was actually heading for oblivion because of a secret George had kept from her. Her trust in him was destroyed. So, too, for the moment, was her faith in herself.

Yet at the same time, Mary Ellen felt sorry for George. Although it was he who terminated the marriage, he was a sensitive and caring man, and it was apparent to Mary Ellen that he too was suffering tremendous emotional stress. Although they now lived apart, they remained partners in the small neighborhood bookstore they'd started together twelve years earlier. For practical business reasons, they just couldn't avoid seeing each other every day, at least until they could sell the store or find a new partner to buy one of them out. So Mary Ellen knew how broken up George felt—she saw how he avoided her eyes, turning away from her to hide his tears.

Ironically enough, Mary Ellen felt somehow responsible for relieving George's misery. She wanted to soothe him, to reassure him that everything was going to be all right. But doing so, I told her, would just distract her from getting on with handling her own problems. While it was helpful for her to understand what George was going through, she had to realize she wasn't his caretaker anymore; she couldn't make everything all better for him.

George had made his decision; now he had to learn to live with it and take care of himself, just as Mary Ellen had to learn to take care of herself. In the end, it would be far better for both of them.

FEAR NO. 1: ECONOMIC FEAR

However troubling or unexpected it may be, your ex's behavior toward you is likely to be rooted in certain fears—some more legitimate than others, but most of them quite comprehensible. One of the most common fears is economic: not having enough money to survive.

This fear is especially pervasive in the aftermath of separation. There are very practical reasons for it. Virtually everyone, whatever their economic status, undergoes a serious disruption in lifestyle after separating. You find yourself living much closer to the line financially. You experience a drop in your comfort level around what you can afford, whether it's for basic items like groceries and clothing, or relative luxuries such as entertainment and eating out. For some, adopting a bare-bones budget means hamburger instead of steak; for others, it means macaroni and cheese instead of hamburger.

Economic fear afflicts men and women alike. And it can severely affect their attitudes and behavior toward each other by turning formerly civil ex-spouses into desperate rivals, battling for their "fair share" of a suddenly inadequate pie. There's always less money to go around for both, and seldom "enough" for either.

Although women are still more likely to end up getting the big assets, such as the house and car—especially if they have custody of children—they typically find their monthly income inadequate to keep the household running as it used to. This is something for ex-husbands to keep in mind. Statistics consistently show that, on average, men fare much better financially than women a few years after the divorce. Women are aware of this reality; if your ex-wife is making what seem like excessive and unreasonable demands, she may be acting out of justifiable economic fear.

This fear doesn't necessarily justify all her demands, of course, but it helps to explain why she's acting that way. You don't have to react in kind by getting into a power struggle and making unreasonable demands of your own. If you can understand that your ex-wife is experiencing terrible anxiety about making ends meet, then it will be easier for you or your lawyer to make a constructive counterproposal. It's often said that a fair separation agreement or divorce settlement is a compromise that leaves neither party entirely satisfied.

JERRY AND MONICA

A patient whom I'll call Jerry felt desperate after his wife, Monica, left him. A line technician for the telephone company, Jerry remained with the two children, nine and eleven, in the ranch-style bungalow that he and Monica had built on five acres in the country. Jerry had had a severe drinking problem for several years—one of the reasons why Monica, feeling pretty desperate herself, had moved to a small apartment in the nearest town. He felt even more depressed when he discovered that Monica was seeing another man. Soon Jerry began talking about killing himself.

Late one night, his eleven-year-old son found him sitting in the living room, an almost-empty bottle of bourbon in one hand and a large bottle of sleeping pills in the other. Once again, Jerry was mumbling about ending it all. The terrified boy called the police, and that was how Jerry ended up seeing me.

In the course of therapy, it turned out that Jerry had yet another big problem: He could no longer afford to keep up the mortgage payments on the property. Without two incomes, there was just no way he could hold onto the place he'd worked so hard to build, especially now that Monica was demanding shared custody of the kids and a chunk of money to set up a household in town.

Although he was paralyzed with fear, Jerry had refused to see a lawyer about negotiating a settlement. He was afraid he'd lose his country place—practically the last thing he felt he had going for him. Meanwhile, Monica, angry with what she regarded as his stubbornness and meanness, and at the same time intimidated by his threats of suicide, began thinking about kidnaping the children.

Finally, I talked Jerry into visiting both a lawyer and a bank manager, to see what could be done about his financial dilemma. Together they found a creative solution: The property was desirable, and large enough that it could be subdivided. Jerry could sell off two two-acre parcels to a builder, leaving himself the house on a single acre of land.

Eventually, by splitting the proceeds from the land sale, Jerry and Monica were able to resolve both their situations. She ended up with a decent settlement, which allowed her to reestablish herself in a new life; he was able to pay down the principal on his mortgage, making his monthly payments manageable. With these arrangements, Jerry, who had been in severe emotional turmoil, was able to get beyond his suicidal urges, and he and Monica ended up agreeing to joint custody of the children.

There are two lessons here. One is the value of obtaining good professional advice on financial and legal matters. The other is the power that economic fear can wield over people. If Monica had realized earlier how this fear had paralyzed Jerry, she wouldn't have assumed that he was refusing to see a lawyer simply because he was a big macho bully who wanted to keep everything for himself, leaving her with nothing. In reality, rather than acting from a position of power, he was reacting from fear.

As we saw from Jerry's behavior, economic fear can entail a great deal more than money lust. In a separation, money takes on tremendous symbolic importance. It's all wrapped up with fundamental questions of personal identity: "What kind of life will I lead now? Where will I live? What will I eat? What clothes will I wear?"

On a practical level, these aren't unreasonable questions. If you've enjoyed a comfortable life-style, you probably won't be able to maintain it at the same level—at least, not for a few years, or as long as it takes to get back on your feet financially. If you're a woman, and especially if you have children, the chances are statistically greater that you'll suffer economically. Surveys consistently show that nearly half of all families headed by single mothers live below the poverty line, while over half of divorced men—upwards of eighty percent in some jurisdictions—default partially or completely on their support payments. The prospect of poverty can be highly threatening for anyone.

BILL'S STORY

The problem of defaulting on payments is so widespread that even our superresponsible friend Bill ran into it. This seemed paradoxical at the time: After all, Bill still felt a strong need to continue supporting and protecting his family after Marie threw him out. Basically an honest man, he didn't stint on the amount of his support payments; I even had to persuade him to retain a lawyer to represent his interests in negotiating the divorce settlement. And as we saw in the last chapter, Bill cared deeply about his son and daughter, even though he had to learn how to slow down and enjoy the time he spent with them on weekends.

Yet a few months after their separation, Marie had to send her lawyer after Bill's lawyer because she wasn't receiving her monthly checks on time. The money would get there eventually, but not soon enough to cover the substantial mortgage payments on the matrimonial home, which were due on the first of the month. So Marie's lawyer demanded postdated checks from Bill to save Marie further trouble with the mortgage company.

Bill was furious. "What the hell's the matter with her?" he fumed. "Doesn't she trust me? Haven't I always met my obligations? I've never welshed on a deal in my life!"

Bill considered Marie's behavior harassment. She was being unreasonably aggressive and hostile toward him, trying to demean him in front of everybody. It wasn't fair, after everything he'd put up with.

After hearing Bill out, and empathizing with how bad he was feeling, I reminded him that his monthly support payments were different from the accounts payable in his carpet business, where he could take a little extra time to pay his suppliers because they knew his credit was good. Marie needed to receive that money on time every month, or she and the children risked being evicted from their home. They had a right to the security of knowing that wasn't going to happen; that security was part of the settlement.

Marie acknowledged that Bill was a decent and generous guy; she also knew that he could get awfully busy at the store doing a hundred things at once, and end up neglecting his bills. At one time, she'd helped him keep his books, so she knew how disorganized he could be. There was thus some basis for her fear.

After working through his defensiveness and anger, Bill conceded that Marie's anxiety was justified, and she wasn't just being a whining, nagging, grasping wife. He wrote out postdated checks for a full year, his anger subsided, and he felt better about the whole incident.

There are seldom "winners" in a divorce settlement. Many ex-spouses who provide support can feel, at least a little, like they're being taken to the cleaners. You should allow for that feeling in your ex-partner or yourself—although it doesn't mean you should surrender your legitimate demands.

Similarly, most ex-spouses receiving support payments are going to feel that they've settled for less money than they need. Consequently, they or their lawyers will often start the bidding high.

If you're a man whose ex starts off by demanding the house, the car, and 125 percent of your salary, you need to realize two things: First, she's not going to get that much, and second, she's probably trying to protect herself because she's insecure, and frightened of what the future will bring. If you take those things into account on receiving that nasty letter from her lawyer, you won't feel as if you're being raped and pillaged on the spot, and you won't need to defend yourself by lashing out in kind. Instead, you can refer the letter to your own lawyer, who will calmly explain your rights and your expectations from a settlement, allowing you to get your feelings under control and to respond with a reasonable counterproposal. Remember, you're in a negotiation.

If no financial support is required by either party, and there are relatively few assets to divide, negotiations may not be necessary. When they are necessary, however, separating partners should avoid haggling in person with each other over terms. You'll both just end up playing out your old adolescent roles one more time, in a grotesque caricature of your dead relationship. You have legal representation for just this reason: to save yourself some grief.

Even after a settlement is reached, the person making support payments may feel "cheated." Are those monthly checks really going to house, feed, and clothe little Johnny? Or is Johnny's mother using the money to buy herself clothes and to have a good time? It's helpful if the person writing the checks can see what the hidden child-rearing costs are. For example, renting a two- or three-bedroom apartment costs substantially more than a one-bedroom; Johnny's appetite is growing and the grocery bills are rising, and so are the inflationary costs of practically everything else, from kids' clothing to their athletic activities. In the end, the great majority of support payments do go toward the necessities of life, rather than toward frivolous purchases. If more ex-husbands (and a few ex-wives) realized these facts, there would be fewer defaults on support payments.

Why, then, is there so much bitter resentment over paying support, such sullen reluctance? And during the divorce negotiation itself, why is the division of assets often so ugly? Once again, a line from the movie *The War of the Roses* comes to mind: the battle-scarred divorce lawyer's cynical remark that "a civilized divorce is a contradiction in terms."

The obvious explanation for this unpleasantness appears to be meanness, selfishness, and greed. But while that may be true sometimes, there's usually more to it psychologically.

Money, possessions, even children come to stand as substitutes for the dead relationship. Grief and anger over the death of the marriage become transformed into grief and anger over the division of assets, both material and spiritual. People who have invested ten, twenty, or thirty years of their lives in a now-dead relationship want to recoup their investment. They don't want to lose those years. So they try to hang on to the house, or the children, or the Oriental rug, or some piece of bric-a-brac from that wonderful April in Paris of a dozen years ago. Sometimes it gets downright dirty, as with the *Roses*; sometimes just plain silly, as with a couple I knew who couldn't agree about ownership of the dining-room suite—she took the table and two chairs, and he got four chairs and the buffet sideboard.

If you find yourself acting this way, ask yourself whether you're just trying to hang on to what was once good about the relationship. Maybe the answer will make it possible to arrive at a more reasonable way of handling the situation. Maybe it will become a little easier to let go.

FEAR NO. 2:
FEAR OF BEING HURT AGAIN

Earlier in this chapter, we met Mary Ellen, whose twenty-nine-year marriage to George ended when he announced he'd come to terms with the fact that he was gay. In the aftermath of their separation, they saw each other almost daily because of their partnership in their small store. George was perfectly willing to discuss business with Mary Ellen, but she couldn't understand why he refused to sit down and discuss their personal relationship, past or future. Why did he want nothing more to do with her on an intimate level? Had she become so repugnant to him? Once again, she felt wounded by George—rejected and hurt.

In fact, Mary Ellen had a hidden agenda: She was hoping that by going over their difficulties, she could win George back. But that had nothing to do with his avoidance of her. George was unable to talk about the relationship because he simply found the subject too painful and sad. He was also afraid Mary Ellen would say hurtful things to him—things she might well have a right to say, but which he didn't want to hear. Right then, he had as much pain as he could bear. He was afraid of being hurt again.

In the early, acute phase of being separated—the deep black pit—people feel so raw, so tender, that mere contact with the ex-partner may be unbearable. They're like burn victims; the only treatment may be to avoid direct contact.

If someone has been physically or psychologically abused, it's obvious why he or she wouldn't want to communicate with the abuser. But if you've behaved reasonably toward your ex, and he or she still refuses to see you or talk things over, it could be due to fear of what you might say.

When you harbor no ill intent toward your ex-partner, his or her reluctance to talk can be confusing or frustrating; it seems arrogant and unfair. But for the time being, you may just have to accept the necessity of communicating through lawyers—or not at all—until your ex is feeling less vulnerable.

CAROL'S STORY

Remarkably enough, even Carol encountered this reaction in her ex-husband, Richard. It happened about six months after they'd separated. By that point, enough time had elapsed for Carol to feel better about herself and her life. As we've seen in previous chapters, she'd gone through a couple of relationships since Richard, and had learned to start meeting her own adult needs.

When Carol attended a conference where Richard was also going to be present (they worked in related fields), she was thus quite prepared to run into him at the various sessions and social functions. She was especially looking forward to the closing reception and dinner, where she'd have a chance to meet and socialize with interesting colleagues.

To Carol's surprise, however, Richard didn't feel comfortable at all about encountering *her*. In fact, he felt quite the opposite. After the work sessions at the conference, he didn't attend any of the social functions. He stayed away from the cocktail parties, the hospitality suites, even the closing dinner—which was unlike him, since normally he liked to win friends and influence people.

Carol was astonished when she found out the reason for Richard's behavior: He was reluctant to confront her socially, fearing it would be painful. He didn't know what to say to her anymore, how to behave. Carol was puzzled: Hadn't Richard been the one who'd wanted out of their marriage? Hadn't he moved right in with his girlfriend, Gwen, whom he'd been keeping secret from Carol? Hadn't he always been the "strong" one?

Carol realized that Richard was belatedly experiencing many of the agonizing feelings she'd already gone through. He was finally mourning their dead marriage, and it was proving very hurtful for him. At the same time, his relationship with Gwen wasn't turning out as he'd hoped, either. Richard wasn't the all-powerful, invulnerable man Carol had imagined—he was human after all.

FEAR NO. 3: SEXUAL FEAR

We all experience some sense of failure when a marriage or relationship dies: a feeling of dashed hopes, of unfulfilled potential. That feeling extends to the sexual realm also—especially if sex between you both was once good. As in everything else about the original relationship, its erotic side is dead, and that can be difficult to accept at first.

If you feel regret over the loss of your sexual partnership, you can assume your ex does too. That sense of loss may give rise to sexual fears: "Am I frigid, as he claimed I was?" "Am I as insensitive and unfeeling as she said?" "Can I still attract the opposite sex?" "Can I perform?" Your ex-partner may be feeling some of these doubts. What's more, he or she may be tempted to act on them—with others, or even with you.

Ideally, sexual matters "shouldn't" be part of any continuing relationship the two of you may have. It would be so much neater that way. But reality is seldom neat and tidy.

If you're meeting to discuss division of assets or child-care responsibilities, and your former partner throws in some gratuitous comments about a new girlfriend or boyfriend, the motive is probably just what you suspect—to make you jealous. Underlying that motive, in turn, is the desire to shore up his or her injured sexual self-image.

When people feel rejected sexually, they naturally fear it will happen again. Flaunting new lovers is one way to prove—to others but also to themselves—that they're still sexually attractive. Another way is to behave seductively. For example, he invites you to a romantic candlelight dinner at Luigi's. Or when you return the kids to the matrimonial home, she meets you at the door in a plunging neckline. It feels like courting again, and it can be tempting to respond in kind—to try to rekindle the erotic flame and recapture what was once a vibrant part of your life together.

At such moments, you must remember where your relationship

stands in reality. You're not courting, so what's really going on? You have to ask yourself if your ex's seductiveness actually means he or she wants you back, or if he/she is just trying to rebuild shaky self-esteem by proving to him- or herself, in an adolescent fashion, that he/she can exert sexual power over you. If you question the motives, you're less likely to be drawn into sexual gamesmanship with your ex. It's not your job to reassure your ex how wonderfully desirable he/she still is.

If you and your former partner end up in bed in the middle of divorce proceedings, you won't be the first couple to do so, nor the last. And the experience may not be particularly disastrous: Who knows, you both may even decide you want to be together after all. But, more typically, the experience will be counterproductive. It muddies the emotional waters, at a time when you need to get clear about the true state of the relationship. It isn't helpful to resume sexual relations when you're proceeding toward a divorce, because you're denying the fact that the relationship is over. You're fostering illusions, stirring up false hopes.

Let's be pragmatic here. Going to bed with your ex tends to be just another pitfall. In fact, it's a variation on pitfall number two, "The Wrong Face," from Chapter 3.

And consider the possibility that amorous former spouses may just be looking to revive rusty romantic skills. Before discovering if they still have what it takes to seduce *anyone*, they'll try it out on you. After all, they had success with you once before.

FEAR NO. 4: FEAR OF BEING ALONE

After years of being in a relationship, separated men and women often find it unnerving to live alone. As we've seen, they may resort to various antidotes for anxiety and loneliness—workaholism, drinking, drugs, sleeping around. If your ex is doing any of these things, his or her behavior may worry or upset you—but that doesn't mean you have to respond by "fixing" it, or by becoming emotionally involved in what your ex is doing.

My patient Brian had to learn this. During the first year after his separation from Fiona, he counted no fewer than five different men who passed through her life. Fiona announced each affair as it began, implying that *this* was the new love of her life. But each time, the romance seemed to fizzle after a few weeks, and she was soon on to the next relationship.

Brian found these affairs traumatic, even though he seldom met the men concerned. He felt Fiona "paraded" her lovers in front of him to wound him—and boy, was she succeeding! He was disgusted and furious. He felt she was not only taunting him, but doing harm to herself. Yet he didn't know how to help her without appearing to be motivated by jealousy or insecurity or self-interest. And although he really didn't want to involve himself in Fiona's private life, he worried over the effect of her affairs on their four-year-old daughter, who lived with her.

The more I learned about Fiona's behavior, the clearer it became that her affairs resulted more from a terror of living alone than from any deliberate attempt to "get" Brian. The pain she was inflicting on him was a by-product of her insensitivity to his feelings, rather than some cruel campaign of revenge. The fact was, she had a compulsion to fill the void in her life with male companionship. Once Brian saw this, he could accept her behavior more easily. Fiona wasn't some sleazy slut out to humiliate him, but a frightened woman who couldn't cope with living alone. And that was *her* problem.

Needless to say, men may act the very same way as Fiona. Some ex-husbands would rather have anybody to come home to than live alone.

FEAR NO. 5: FEAR OF CHILD-REARING

Assuming responsibility for raising children can be daunting for some newly separated people. If you've always viewed child-rearing as a shared activity that takes place within the warm, protective confines of a nuclear family, having to raise a child alone can seem like an ominous responsibility. This can lead to making huge issues out of relatively small matters to do with the kids, or taking parental responsibilities so seriously that they blot out other concerns and interests. If your ex is fearful and apprehensive about child-rearing, it can have an impact on you as well as the children.

For example, Kim's ex-husband, Mike, a burly policeman and former semipro football player, was a capable guy in many ways, but a nervous klutz around their three-year-old daugher, Alanna. Kim knew Mike loved his daughter, yet in four months of separation, he hadn't offered to take Alanna for a single overnight visit, and Alanna was heartbroken. "Daddy doesn't love me!" she wailed. This naturally upset Kim; she worried about the impact on Alanna of not having contact with her father.

I suggested that Kim talk this problem over with Mike, as frankly and as calmly as she could. If he realized the effect of his behavior on Alanna, maybe he'd do something about it.

To Kim's relief, Mike confessed that he longed to have Alanna visit with him, but he was afraid he wouldn't be able to provide the care she needed: feeding her, doing her hair, dressing her. The fact was that, during their marriage, Kim had done all the child-rearing. Mike had been left out of that experience, and now felt incapable of handling it on his own.

Kim quickly gave Mike the simple tips he needed to know about caring for his child. It wasn't as hard as he thought, Kim assured him, and if he got into difficulties, he could always call her for advice. This made Mike feel a whole lot more confident and willing to try a visit, and Alanna soon began seeing more of her dad.

This illustrates how readily you can apply common sense to a problem when you understand what's really going on with your ex-partner. But when you don't understand his or her fears, the problem appears much more complicated and upsetting: Motives are misunderstood; the misunderstandings multiply; hostility is compounded. The same is true with other kinds of feelings—anger, for example.

VARIOUS ANGERS

To one degree or another, conflict is inevitable between separating or divorcing partners; inevitably, both parties will feel and express their anger. Part of handling your ex's anger is learning a little self-defense.

There are a host of things your ex could, and probably is, angry about—and that's fine. The bottom line is that his or her anger isn't your problem anymore. I mean, there have to be *some* benefits to splitting up; one of them is that you don't have to soothe, placate, or defuse the other's angry feelings.

If your former spouse tries to foist his/her anger onto you, you're under no obligation to accept it. You can say, "That's something your lawyer can take up with my lawyer." Or you can say, "Why don't you discuss that with your therapist (or friend)?" Or simply, "I don't want to talk about it."

After the separation or divorce agreement is settled, there's usually little reason for ongoing interaction unless you have kids. And even then, you can say, "I'll discuss it if it's about the kids. Otherwise, I'm not interested." As a last resort, you can hang up the telephone or walk out the door. If you're at home, you can ask your ex to leave. If he or she refuses, you can call the police.

Some of this anger emerges, as we saw earlier, because the relationship is dead. But if you get drawn into the conflict process, you're colluding with your ex in keeping the dead relationship artificially alive with infusions of anger. You don't need to get drawn in, although you may feel very tempted. It happens a lot, especially in the acute grieving phase right after separation. Some people keep the anger—and hence the crippled, conflict-ridden relationship—going for years.

When this happens, it's really another form of power struggle. You can "win" it by refusing to participate in the conflict. You have better things to do.

The litany of angry complaints may include:

- anger over being disillusioned with the relationship, being emotionally "cheated"
- anger over being rejected or abandoned
- anger over being financially disadvantaged
- anger over being "tied down" by children

This last anger is especially pernicious, and deserves special comment here. It's awfully easy to feel angry at the kids just for being there, at a time when everything's so tough for you. After all, they cost you plenty in time and money; they cramp your lifestyle and freedom; they're an emotional drain.

People tell me, "It would be so different if I didn't have kids."

And I reply, "So it would. Life would be different for all of us if we didn't have kids."

It's important not to take out your anger on the children. If your ex does it, without bad-mouthing him or her, you can point out to the kids, "Mom (or Dad) is really angry right now because of our breakup, and you're getting some of the fallout."

More about children in the next chapter.

Chapter Six

What Your Children Need From You

When reflecting on the impact of separation and divorce on children, I think of the time I told my son and daughter why I was writing this book. I explained to them that going through a separation is always difficult; that adults are sad and hurting then, and I hoped to write a book that would help them through a bad time.

My explanation wasn't really needed. My son replied, "Yeah, we know—it happened to *us*, remember?"

His comment is a useful reminder of a basic truth: The breakup of a marriage affects the children as much as the parents. They feel the pain, too. It may be different from ours, but it can be just as powerful emotionally. As parents, we need to understand how the experience feels from their perspective.

With nearly half of all marriages now breaking up, there are lots of children of divorce out there. But that doesn't mean kids consider it "normal" for their parents' marriage to end, even if many of their friends are in single-parent families. When couples are having difficulties, or fighting frequently, their children may ask apprehensively, "Does this mean you and Daddy are going to get divorced?" They've heard about it; they've seen it on television; they've watched it happen to their friends—and they don't want it to happen to *them*. Even if their family has problems, they would rather cling to the world they know. As most of us do, they fear the unknown.

LETTING CHILDREN HAVE THEIR EMOTIONS

Right after separation or divorce, kids are sad for a time. Their sadness hurts us too, and makes us want to do something to eliminate their pain. But we have to remember they have a right to their sadness, and to any other feelings they may be experiencing, including anger. After all, the world as they've always known it has ended.

From most children's point of view, living with both parents—even if half the kids at school don't—is the natural order of things. When that order is disrupted, it opens up a whole spectrum of unknowns.

So you can expect children to react with anxiety and fear, as well as sadness and anger—but you can comfort and reassure them, too. You can help them get through this time by being:

1. *Consistent*—making your relationship with them as predictable and reliable as you can.
2. *Loving*—showing them, through actions as well as words, how much you care for them.
3. *Reassuring*—telling them, in no uncertain terms, that even though their parents have separated, Mommy and Daddy both still love them, and will both still be there for them—and backing up those statements by promoting a good relationship between them and the absent parent.

By taking this approach, your children will have a good chance of working through their anxieties and learning to accept the new reality in their lives. But as you did, they'll need time to mourn their old life before accepting the new one—even if the new one's going to be better.

In the meantime, you'll have to be honest with them about the permanence of your marriage breakup. Most children entertain at least some hopes and fantasies that Mom and Dad will get back together again. They may cling to these hopes and fantasies for a surprisingly long time—especially if neither parent is involved in a stable relationship with someone else. If that finally happens, the children are usually able to say, "You know, I can't imagine you and Dad (Mom) living together anymore—you're both so different."

Until then, you can expect your kids to indulge in reconciliation fantasies. And that's all right, if it gives them a temporary handhold on the security they need. Just remember that you don't need to act out their fantasies for them. After all, you don't act out all your *own* fantasies—why should you feel an obligation to act out someone else's?

Here's where an important maxim comes in: You're not responsible *to* your children, you're responsible *for* them.

Your real responsibility is to provide adequate and appropriate parenting. This means that when your child verbalizes the fantasy—"Daddy, why don't you and Mommy get together again?"—you respond from your own adult experience, and not from the child's experience. You say, "I know you'd like that to happen. But your Mommy and I just can't live together anymore. It wouldn't work out for us—and it wouldn't work out for you either."

Exactly how you say it depends, of course, on your children's ages, maturity, and personalities. By acknowledging their wish, while at the same time clarifying that it isn't going to come true, you are recognizing their inner reality and showing that you're responsible for making the tough but necessary decisions.

As for *why* your marriage broke up, you'll want to give your children some sort of explanation—again, appropriate to their age level—when they ask, as they inevitably will. Make it brief but clear, so they won't feel completely left in the dark. And keep it honest, but not *too* honest: Leave out the gory details.

If for example, you say something like, "We just grew apart," it will be fairly meaningless to them. On the other hand, avoid:

"Your father is a despicable swine," or "Your mother is a conniving bitch," since it doesn't help your kids to hear you bad-mouthing their other parent.

You might try some variation on: "Your mother (father) and I just can't live together anymore . . . . We were very unhappy with each other, fighting about things all the time . . . . We tried counseling [provided you actually did], and it didn't work for us . . . . So it's best if we live apart now. And believe it or not, it's best for you too."

Those are about all the lines I can feed you. In fielding your kids' questions, I'm afraid you're on your own. The only real ground rules I would suggest are to avoid character assassination, and especially, to avoid explicit sexual issues; certainly with younger children, and even with teenagers. In general, it's not a good idea for kids to know too much about their parents' sex lives. That would just involve them inappropriately with intimate details that would disturb them, which are none of their business anyway.

WINNING AT THE CRAPSHOOT OF LIFE

As parents, we can't help but worry how our children will be affected by the marriage breakup. Sometimes we agonize so much that we stay in a relationship that's wrong for us, for fear of what might happen to the kids if the marriage ends.

Parents should know that children of divorce don't have to turn out badly—far from it. Studies have shown that kids from unhappy homes, where the parents stayed together (often "for the sake of the children"), are just as likely to be adversely affected as kids from divorced homes. Whether you're a married, separated, or divorced mom or dad, it's important to remember you still exert a powerful, positive influence on the way your kids cope emotionally and develop psychologically.

In reality, kids are capable of doing just fine, despite the fact that their parents have split up. How well the kids deal with the situation depends on how their parents handle it. Just because you're separated or divorced doesn't mean you abdicate your responsibilities as a parent. Sometimes, of course, you may wonder why you ever had kids in the first place! But the fact is, you did—so you continue to bear parental responsibilities for them. It doesn't follow, however, that you're stuck with staying married to their other parent.

Ultimately, the major factor in determining how children of divorce turn out is the ongoing involvement in their lives of *both* parents. Whether you or your ex have sole custody of the child(ren), or whether you have joint or shared custody, the cardinal point is that there should be continuing, consistent contact between *each* of you and the kids. If you can manage that, your children will stand a better chance of growing up emotionally stable—more so than either children who have had no contact with one parent, or children whose parents have stayed together in bad marriages.

There are two other benefits from having both parents involved with the children. One is that, of necessity, there is more constructive cooperation and mutual support between ex-spouses, making life easier and more pleasant for everybody. The other advantage is that noncustodial parents—typically fathers—are far more likely to keep up support payments when their kids are a continuing, regular presence in their lives.

The prejudice that children of "broken homes" always turn out badly dies hard. But in fact, if they're loved, nurtured, and well cared for, they have as good a chance in the crapshoot of life as any other child.

RESHAPING THE PARENT-CHILD RELATIONSHIP

Just as in traditional nuclear families, raising a child as a single parent requires work, devotion, and sensitivity. Part of that effort involves reshaping your relationship with your child, establishing a different kind of connection from the one you both had when you and your ex-spouse were together. Sometimes, it can be an even stronger, better connection.

Your objective is to encourage and assist your children toward having two good but *separate* relationships with their natural parents. Until you've achieved that objective, it's natural to worry about what's going to happen to your relationship with your children. You might even be tempted, as was one of my patients, to do something that's wrong for *you*, in an attempt to please or placate them.

That patient, Anna, had a husband who cheated on her incessantly, yet always expected her indulgence and forgiveness. Finally refusing to be treated any longer as a combination doormat and den mother, Anna told him to leave. A few weeks later he came crawling back, acting like a chastened little boy and pleading to be allowed to return home.

Anna had heard his protestations of "love" and promises of "good" behavior too often to be taken in again. She'd been hurt and humiliated enough. Yet she wavered in her resolve, partly because her teenage children, missing their father, put pressure on Anna to be "nice" and let him return. She was afraid that if she didn't agree, the children would accuse her of cruelty and side with her husband, and her relationship with them would be irretrievably damaged.

Anna was put in a difficult and unfair position: forced to choose between what was good for her and what was supposedly good for someone else. But in fact, she wouldn't have been doing any favor to her insensitive egomaniac of a husband to let him think he could continue abusing her emotionally. Equally important, the children couldn't be allowed to exercise such power—really a form of emotional blackmail—over their mother.

I had to remind Anna that we're responsible *for* our children, but not *to* them. The only person she was responsible to was herself. At the time, she was having difficulty seeing what life would be like six months down the road, when her relationship with her kids would gradually become stronger. In the meantime, she had to endure their disapproval, and trust that they'd come around to seeing she wasn't being unreasonable after all. If she had behaved in a destructive and irrational manner, I told her, then the children would have reason to see her that way; but she hadn't. And indeed, they finally came to accept the validity of her position. They even began standing up for her to their father—but only after Anna had begun standing up for herself. Her relationship with them weathered the storm, and evolved into a more candid, open, and loving connection than before.

PREDICTABILITY, CONSISTENCY, RELIABILITY

When dealing with children of any age, but especially younger ones, a vital principle to keep in mind is the need for predictability and consistency in their lives. This is especially true in the aftermath of their parents' breakup, when they're feeling uncertain and anxious. You can help them by providing some certainties for them to hold onto while they adjust to a new way of life. For example, regarding visits from the noncustodial parent, you can inform the kids when the visits are going to happen, then stick by it.

If you're the noncustodial parent: When you tell your children you're going to visit them every Saturday, take them for dinner on Wednesdays, or have them at your place every other weekend, then that's exactly what you should do. The frequency doesn't matter as much as the predictability, consistency, and reliability of your contact with them. Your children need to be able to count on you to be there when you said you would.

If you're the custodial parent: Once you've both arrived at a mutually agreeable arrangement, it's vital that you support and facilitate your ex's visits with the kids. Try not to sabotage those plans, consciously or unconsciously. It will only hurt your children, and it certainly won't help you either.

Rosa, a hard-nosed negotiator for a labor union, took her ex-husband back to court after a big blowup with him over his visits with their nine-year-old son. She wanted to revise their divorce agreement, and abolish her ex's visitation rights, because he was always late arriving to pick the boy up. Their agreement had provided for the traditional "reasonable access" by the father, but Rosa considered it unreasonable that he was often twenty minutes to an hour late. The last straw came when he made her and her boyfriend late for a dinner party one night. That sort of embarrassment wouldn't happen, she insisted, if she could just hire a babysitter and forget about her ex-husband's rights.

I agreed with Rosa that, yes, being late was unreasonable; and yes, the man had been chronically unpunctual all the years she'd known him; and yes, it had always bugged the hell out of her.

But I had to remind her that he was still her son's father, and that denying him access to his son wouldn't be helpful—quite the opposite. In the long run, this action would only damage her son, as well as her own relationship with him.

Even though legally Rosa had sole custody, I was willing to bet that if she had continued to deny her ex-husband access to his son, by the time the boy was fifteen, he'd want to move out and live with his dad. This problem often arises when a child idealizes an absent parent. As anyone bringing up a fifteen-year-old knows, your teenager frequently regards you as the worst person in the world. Consequently, it's tempting for the teenager to idealize the absent or distant parent. This is less likely to happen if the child sees the noncustodial parent often enough to realize that this parent isn't perfect either.

Rosa could be as angry as she wanted with her former husband, but by punishing him, she would have punished their son—a big mistake. Fortunately, she saw the sense in this and dropped her suit.

As we saw in the previous chapter, although some ex-partners' behaviors can be irritating or even infuriating, you don't have to get sucked into prolonging the battles of the dead relationship. And, unless there are serious abuses to contend with, it's seldom worth causing a big legal ruckus to the detriment of the children. Don't surrender to the temptation to express your anger at your ex through your kids.

Of course, there's a balance to be struck between making accommodations for the sake of your children (which we all do as parents) and standing up for your own rights and legitimate self-interest. Another female patient of mine went to the opposite extreme from the one just mentioned. Grace never said anything critical about her ex-husband or engaged in any form of conflict with him, because she didn't want to upset her three kids.

The trouble was, this approach worked to her detriment. Her former husband interpreted her reasonableness as weakness and took advantage of it. Eighteen months after the separation, he was nine thousand dollars in arrears on his support payments, and Grace was working night and day at two full-time jobs just to make ends meet. That's how bad her situation had to get before she took legal steps to have the court attach his wages for nonpayment.

Grace finally learned from experience to stop protecting her kids from knowing too much about their father's failings. For example, her twelve-year-old son wanted very badly to play in a sandlot football league—which would require that he be driven long distances several times a week to games and practices. Grace simply had no time free from her two jobs to do the driving, so she told her son he could play as long as he could work out the transportation with his father. Sure, the man said, no problem. Anything for my son, the football player!

Grace kept her fingers crossed; she didn't want the boy to be let down. But sure enough, in this, as in other things, her ex-husband didn't keep his end of the bargain. He failed to get the boy to practices, so the boy missed making the team. Grace hated seeing her son so disappointed and hurt, but at the same time, she couldn't continue covering up his father's irresponsibility forever. Thus her son learned what his father really was made of. If this man wanted to start having an authentic relationship with his kid, he'd have to work at it a lot harder. It was his problem, not hers.

YOU CAN'T ALWAYS GET WHAT YOU WANT

A mistake many single parents make is assuming their children should have things—toys, clothing, sports activities, lessons—that the parents really can't afford to provide.

Often, these "should haves" are highly unrealistic. When the child asks for something, the parent responds out of a sense of guilt, instead of making a judgment about whether or not the child genuinely needs this item. Such parents may forget that it's normal and natural for children not to have everything they want. Even in a conventional, two-parent family, children don't—and shouldn't—have their every wish fulfilled, their every whim gratified.

Take the case of Bill, whose progress we've been following in previous chapters. Bill had always tended to overplay his provider role, so it bothered him when he found that supporting two households and a business was straining his pocketbook, and that he had to cut back on his "nothing but the best" approach to his daughter, Lisa, and son, Jordan. Even after he had to go to the bank for a personal loan, he felt guilty that he could no longer afford to buy the Nintendo game Jordan wanted, or the "right"—and overpriced—designer clothes for Lisa. He imagined this made him somehow inadequate as a father.

The truth was that, deep down, Bill was feeling guilty about the failure of his marriage and its effect on the children. He was afraid they'd be angry with him for not keeping the family intact. If he didn't get Jordan that Nintendo game, maybe Jordan wouldn't love him anymore; if Lisa wasn't the spiffiest little dresser in her seventh-grade class, she'd feel horribly deprived, and would take it out on Dad.

It took Bill a while to discard these cockeyed notions—and to accept the reality that children's love isn't bought with material possessions. So what if they didn't have the latest video games, or the right labels on their clothes? Even if he and Marie had stayed together, sooner or later they'd have had to draw the line on materialism somewhere.

More broadly, Bill had to stop compensating for his guilt feelings by trying to make everything rosy for his kids. This issue came into focus through an incident involving Jordan at school. As a gesture of individualism, Jordan had taken to wearing his favorite hat in class. Unamused, his teacher abruptly snatched the hat off Jordan's head one day and refused to return it to him. When Jordan protested, he was sent to the principal's office.

Jordan told the principal his side of the story: There was another boy who had permission to wear a hat in class, so why couldn't he? Jordan was angry, convinced that his rights were being infringed upon and that he was a victim of discrimination.

Calmly, the principal explained that the other boy had been very ill during the summer holidays; he'd undergone chemotherapy, so he'd received permission to wear a hat to conceal his hair loss. Realizing the gravity of his classmate's situation, and feeling foolish he hadn't understood, Jordan broke down and cried. It was such an emotional scene that the principal phoned both Marie and Bill, just to let them know what had happened.

Bill was upset when he heard about the incident. His gut reaction was to rush in and deal with the issue—to protect Jordan somehow, to tell that teacher óff, to give that principal a piece of his mind for mistreating his son. But Jordan was adamant that his father should stay out of it. It was over now, Jordan said, and he could live with the result.

I told Bill that this was just how the incident should end. It was natural enough that Jordan had broken down crying, frustrated with himself for losing his first big confrontation with authority. But he'd survived the confrontation and was stronger for having dealt with it on his own. Bill had assumed the tears meant Jordan was still unhappy about the marriage breakup; he was still interpreting his son's behavior in the light of his own guilt feelings. After this, Bill realized Jordan would encounter other problems as he grew up, and Bill didn't have to feel responsible for causing—or solving—every last one of them.

CUSTODY ARRANGEMENTS

So far, in this chapter, we've been looking primarily at emotional, psychological, and ethical issues of child-rearing after separation. Now it's time to consider the legal basis underlying these issues—the kinds of agreements that ex-spouses make for custody and care of their children.

There are three basic types of custody arrangements: sole, joint, or shared custody.

Sole custody: Traditionally, this has been the commonest way of assigning responsibility for child care after divorce. The custodial parent retains sole legal authority for the major decisions regarding the education, home life, and upbringing of the children. The noncustodial parent normally receives visitation rights on the basis of "reasonable access," but cedes the primary parenting responsibility to the ex-spouse. Formerly, mothers nearly always received sole custody, but that pattern is changing. Now, as gender roles become more flexible; as fathers take more direct involvement in parenting; and as women become more career-oriented and financially independent, fathers are beginning to receive sole custody more frequently than in the past.

Joint custody: This generally means that the children live primarily with one parent, as above, but both parents have joint legal rights in arriving at major decisions regarding their kids' lives and welfare: for example, which schools they'll attend; when and where they'll spend vacations; whether and where to send them to camp, to an orthodontist, or whatever. Joint custody demands a reasonable degree of consultation, cooperation, and common values between ex-spouses.

Shared custody: Demanding an even higher degree of cooperation and good will, this arrangement entails an equal sharing of responsibility for, and time with, the children. They live half the time with each parent. The time cycle can vary widely: half-weeks, alternate weeks, every two weeks, or alternate months. Even alternate years has been practiced successfully.

Assuming some goodwill exists between separating parents, I encourage them to work out, at the very minimum, a joint-custody arrangement. Earlier in this chapter, we considered the benefits of equal involvement by both parents. Even if sole custody is preferred, or necessary, I encourage the custodial parent to support the relationship between the children and the other parent—even to share some of the decision making about the children. This will keep the noncustodial parent more involved and committed. And, as we've seen, that's good for both kids and parents.

In cases of sole or joint custody, the decision about where children will reside remains basically with the parents. Of course, if they can't agree, the matter may have to be decided in court. But it's preferable (and cheaper) if separating spouses can arrive at a mutually acceptable decision based on a combination of factors: practicality, convenience, and above all, the best interests of the child.

When children are small, the decision will be the parents' alone. The older the children, the more their preferences become a factor, especially when they've reached their teens and can be expected to sit down with their parents, individually or together, and provide input into the decision. But it's still not their decision alone—no more than a fourteen-year-old has the whole say over which school to attend, or how expensive a bike to buy.

Certainly, kids should never be subjected to the pressure placed on one teenage boy I knew, whose mother and father marched into his room and announced: "We've decided to separate. Now, which one of us do you want to live with?" That's an awful burden of choice to place on a child; he's damned if he does, damned if he doesn't. Most children don't have the experience or maturity to take all the relevant factors into account in deciding what's best for them. Nor should they have to read their parents' minds, or make a judgment about their parents' needs ("Which one of them wants—or needs—me more?"). Decisions about custody are ultimately part of the adults' continuing responsibilities as parents.

THE ONUS IS ON YOU

Noncustodial parents have the responsibility for keeping up their relationship with children who are living with the ex-spouse. Some noncustodial parents get angry when their kids don't call them on the phone: "Don't the little ingrates care? Have they forgotten I exist?" But I always ask: "So why haven't you called them? The onus is on you, not your child."

In the matter of who does the phoning, it's almost always easier for the adult than for the child. Often it's difficult and awkward for the child to phone, especially when relations between ex-spouses are still tense. Whereas, if the parent initiates the call, the child can still have that continuing contact without feeling guilty about "betraying" the other parent.

When I was first separated, prior to establishing a shared-custody agreement with my ex-wife, I used to phone my two kids at 6:00 P.M. every day at their mom's house. They were small then, so the conversations weren't long or detailed. But those chats became part of our daily routine. They were a morale booster for me, and the kids liked them too; they allowed the three of us to have ongoing contact that we could count on. It got so special that my daughter told her friends, "Don't phone me at six, that's when my dad calls."

Another benefit of the daily calls was that I knew what was happening in their lives. This even took some of the parenting pressure off my ex-wife, since I, too, had to listen to the kids' problems and complaints and help deal with them.

Whatever the frequency of your phone calls to your children—every day, every other day, once a week—the important thing is that the calls should be predictable and consistent. If you tell your kids you'll call them on Thursday, make sure you follow up and do it. As in all parenting, if we're reliable in our kids' eyes, then we're doing our job and helping to give them a sense of security about the world.

As a psychiatrist, I sometimes find I have to get tough with parents who don't want to deal with their kids any longer: "Every time I spend Sunday with Debbie and have to take her back to her mom, it just breaks my heart. I think I'm going to have to stop seeing her."

And I reply: "Tough bananas. Being a parent hurts now and then. But it's no reason to stop seeing your daughter. That would amount to abandoning her, and abandoning a child is a terrible thing to do."

There's no question that being separated from your children is tough. On brief and inadequate visits, when you have to give up your children at the end of the day, it's like reliving the pain of your original separation all over again. It hurts, all right. But it hurts children far more when a parent refuses to see them.

Separating from a spouse definitely doesn't mean abandoning your children, but refusing to see them *does*. An abandoned child is a child wounded for life. Children of separation and divorce don't have to be wounded. It's up to *both* parents to make sure they aren't.

IS THERE A "BEST" AGE?

Some parents take the opposite tack—staying together "for the sake of the children," until their kids are "old enough" to handle a separation. This may help to explain the increasing incidence of couples who split up in their fifties, after the children are grown up. Is there an age when children are best able to deal with the experience?

People often assume that the emotional impact of separation and divorce is hardest on very young children, who are most helpless and vulnerable. But ironically, research suggests it may be even tougher on teenagers.

Very young children actually have a better chance of maintaining consistent contact with both separated parents. Also, there is plenty of time remaining to redefine the parent-child relationship, and to permit a normal childhood under revised circumstances. But for a fifteen-year-old, there are fewer years remaining in the family home, hence less time to adjust to the separation. And in any case, an adolescent's main developmental task isn't dealing with parents as much as moving beyond them and into the world of peers and community.

In the process of learning to become adults, teenagers need to be able to rebel against home and parents. But to do that, they need home and parents to *be* there, even in separate households. They need home to be a relatively stable base camp, where they can drop in from time to time to eat, sleep, and do a little homework. If the base camp breaks up, it can interrupt their development toward adulthood.

Equally, you can wait until Johnny goes off to college, but that can be a "bad" time too. Even if children are in their twenties, even in their thirties or forties, the end of their parents' marriage always causes some emotional upset, some dislocation in feelings and expectations between the generations. From the point of view of children of any age, there is never a "best" time for parents to split up.

One lesson gleaned from all this is that there isn't much to be gained by staying in a miserable marriage for the sake of the children. Yet many people stick around for an extra ten or fifteen years, when they could be getting on with their lives while still meeting their parental responsibilities. Since those responsibilities don't end when the marriage ends, we'll be looking at them some more in later chapters—at later stages in your progress toward living successfully on your own again.

For now, suffice it to say that your job as a single parent is to become the best single parent you can be. You may well have done the best thing for your kids by removing them from a bad or destructive family situation; life may now actually become better for them. As a responsible adult and parent, you'll still do the best you can by your child. Nobody can do more than that.

Stage Three
Becoming You

T he third stage is one of consolidation and expansion: consolidating your gains from the previous stages, and expanding your involvements with people and the world. Whereas Stage Two entailed learning about your adult needs, in Stage Three you can take decisive steps to meet them. Knowing you don't need anyone to take care of you, you can address the question of how to get cared *about* as a person.

This process starts with caring about yourself. We'll be looking at the notion of "constructive selfishness," and also at getting out into the world and meeting people—people you can share with. Some of those people will become your friends. Some may even become intimate friends.

As most of us would agree, you'd probably like to get to this stage a whole lot sooner. Typically, however, most people experience it during Year Two. The whole process takes about a year, and unfolds at its own pace—but it's well worth waiting and working for.

Chapter Seven

At Home With Yourself

I n the last two chapters, we looked at the important tasks of redefining your relationships with your ex-partners and children. Now we're going to look at redefining your relationship with yourself. It's the most important one of all.

This is the point where being on your own again becomes truly rewarding—even exciting.

Before this, you had to go through that horrible, black time at the beginning of your separation, when you just held on to survive from day to day. You grieved over your dead relationship, and grief takes time. Then, groundhog-style, you began to peer out over the edges of your dark emotional pit. You began making forays into the outside world. You took a good look at what your adult needs are, and what you can do to meet them.

Now you can get right out there into the sunshine. You know you're going to survive—so you can look ahead with anticipation, beyond living one day at a time, to a fresh involvement with the world. You can afford to embrace new activities, new enthusiasms, new friendships. You can give rein to your curiosity, your sense of adventure and fun. You can play again.

I see this sense of excitement reborn again and again in patients who've reached this stage. They're thrilled to discover they can do something simply because it feels good. If they have children, they start making good use of the times when their kids are with the other parent. Instead of feeling lonely and abandoned, they think, "Whew, at last I have some space—now there's nobody to be responsible for but me."

There are so many things you can do just for yourself now. It can start with something as simple, for instance, as finding a congenial restaurant or café where you feel comfortable going on your own, where you can get a good meal whenever you don't feel like cooking, or a coffee and croissant while reading the paper on a

Saturday morning. After a while you begin to feel at home there; you get friendly with the staff and other customers; you become one of the regulars. It feels good to have another home base, a place that provides a lively atmosphere and an opportunity to make new friends. After all, you don't meet a whole lot of people if you stay at home. It's nice to know you don't have to feel confined to your four walls.

That's just one small example of learning to get out and do things that are only for your benefit. Now's the time to give yourself permission to do things that are just for you—whether it's going for a nice, long, meandering bike ride by yourself, or choosing to see the movie *you* like, or eating whenever and whatever feels right for you. You can take advantage of your new freedom. You no longer have to travel at someone else's speed.

CONSTRUCTIVE SELFISHNESS

So why are you doing these things? You're doing them just for you—that's reason enough. Strange as it may seem, it's perfectly okay for adults to do something that benefits them and no one else.

When I suggest this to patients, they often look worried. They say, "But, Doctor, isn't that selfish?" And I reply, "Well, yes, as a matter of fact. What's wrong with that?"

Selfishness has been given an undeservedly bad name. Channeled in constructive directions, selfishness can be very healthy.

Even folks who devote themselves to helping the less fortunate will admit, if they're honest, "I do it because it feels good." There's nothing terrible about that. I'm sure Mother Teresa feels very good indeed about her work on behalf of humanity. After all, if what you're always doing *doesn't* feel good, then you're a masochist, and that's pathological.

Far from being "wrong," there's a fundamental necessity for human beings to be "constructively selfish." Looking after our own interests is natural. When you're making sure you're nourished, clothed, and housed, for example, that's "selfish"—and entirely reasonable and necessary. Nobody condemns you for it. Consider the consequences if we didn't look after ourselves: Someone else would have to do it, and we'd wind up being cared for in a treatment facility.

Let's carry this idea a little further. If you don't fill yourself up emotionally, as well as physically, you'll have no energy, nothing to give back to the world. So you need to prime the pump. You need to do things that feel good, that stimulate and satisfy you, even if it's just setting the laundry aside and taking that swim you've been craving, or curling up with a good book you've been dying to read. The laundry can wait till tomorrow!

When you do something constructive, just for you, you feel better. And when you feel better, you're more energetic, more outgoing, and more enjoyable to be with—for others, and for yourself as well. After all, you're spending a lot more time in your own company now. It's more important than ever to feel comfortably at home with yourself.

YOUR NEW RESPONSIBILITIES

Don't take this to mean you no longer have responsibilities. But, as in so many other things, your responsibilities are changing.

Back in Chapter 4, we discussed your two primary adult needs: to be productive, and to be cared about as a person. Meeting those needs will happen only if you first care about yourself as a person. That's a responsibility that doesn't depend on anybody else. When you start caring about yourself, it becomes possible for others to care about you as well—as a separate individual, not as a mere extension of themselves and their own needs.

If that's selfish, so be it. But if nobody cared about themselves, this world would be a pretty sad and depressed place.

What this really means is that you're responsible *for* yourself. And to whom are you responsible? *To* yourself. Period.

People will say, "But aren't we all responsible for each other?"

Not really. Certainly, if you have children below the age of majority, you're responsible for them (but not, as we saw in the previous chapter, to them). And if you have elderly or infirm relatives, you may be responsible for them, too. But you're not responsible for anyone else.

There's only one person you can be responsible *to*—yourself.

So what are you responsible to yourself *for?* For being the best sort of person you can be.

What do I mean by that? I don't mean trying to live up to some ideal of perfection. We can't all be Mother Teresa. And since it's yourself you're answering to, you're the one who determines the sort of person you want to be. Even while caring about others, and respecting them and trying to understand them as much as you can, you still have the right and responsibility to define your own values—your idea of the person you want to be.

In your adolescent marriage or relationship, it was sometimes difficult to know what kind of person you wanted to be, or what your values were. Back then, you were trying so hard to be a good caretaker, and at the same time, a good little boy or girl, that your vision of yourself was blurred.

You went to boring football games because that was what *he* wanted. When you went on big family picnics in the ant-infested countryside, it was *her* idea of a good time. Now you can freely acknowledge that, deep down, you hate football or big family picnics. It's not that you blame your ex for those things—even then, you had the responsibility for doing whatever you wanted. But now, you can freely decide on your own whether or not to do those things—nobody can "make" you.

I'm not taking a totally libertine approach here. I'm not saying you have an absolute, inalienable right to do whatever you damn well please to anybody. I believe there must be reasonable limits on our freedom, so that the rights and the freedom of others are respected. But you do have a right and responsibility to be yourself—no one else can do that for you.

BURYING THE ADOLESCENT RELATIONSHIP

In the give and take of adult relationships, we have to compromise sometimes. But in your adolescent relationship, you probably made *concessions* instead of genuine compromises.

In your adolescent relationship, you might have gone to that football game pretending to be a fan, while deep down you resented the experience the whole time. Or you might have agreed to go on the big family picnic, but you really hated the idea; you sabotaged the occasion by refusing to have a good time, with the result that nobody else had a good time either.

Now that you're an adult exercising free choice, you no longer have to say, as a child says to a parent, "You can make me go, but I won't have a good time." You can go in a positive spirit of enjoyment, as if you'd chosen to go yourself—which, of course, you have. By the same token, you can choose not to go. Either way, you've taken responsibility for your actions.

Emma, a successful real estate agent, was a patient who was very fond of bicycling. Emma wasn't especially athletic, but she did love getting out on a nice day to explore the world on her bike. Her husband, a computer scientist, took a diametrically opposite approach. He did everything superbly: He was a superb scientist, a superb swimmer, a superb cyclist. He practiced the Art of Cycling, whereas Emma just liked "biking around."

Needless to say, going on a ride with her husband was far from fun for Emma. She always had to knock herself out to keep up with him, all the while listening to his instructions about when she ought to be changing gears. He was never interested in slowing down to see the sights, which, as far as Emma was concerned, was the real reason for cycling in the first place.

After her separation, Emma found that one of her greatest pleasures was being free to "bike around" at her own speed. Whenever she felt like it, she would get off her bike and smell the roses, or sit on a park bench and watch the clouds floating past in the blue sky. At those moments, she didn't miss her husband at all. Eventually, Emma realized her bike rides were a symbol of her new freedom to live her way.

In the same vein, Emma discovered a new pleasure in going antiquing on the weekends. By herself, or with a friend who shared her interest in collectibles, she'd explore antique shops or drive the back roads in search of country auctions, just to see if there was anything interesting she could pick up at a good price. She knew her husband would have hated the "aimlessness" of this activity. The wandering, the lack of a defined goal, would have driven him nuts. But Emma loved it, for the very reason that it was spontaneous and open-ended.

In the process, she also discovered she had a passion for wicker furniture. It was a passion she hadn't been quite aware of, until she found herself buying her seventh item—a large, elaborate plant holder to put in the window of the study her husband had vacated. It was a passion she'd never have discovered while she was being responsible to him instead of herself.

Guy, another patient of mine, took up a rather unusual hobby after his separation. Looking for a pursuit of his own that would appeal to his offbeat sense of adventure, Guy settled on flying lessons—but not the usual kind. He decided to learn to fly "ultralights," which are one-seater, lightweight airplanes with small engines that remind me, personally, of a lawnmower engine. Ultralights don't go up very high—just high enough that if you crash, it hurts.

Guy thought that flying these contraptions was the best fun he'd ever had. It was a quiet, solitary activity, requiring intense concentration and close attention to wind currents, and so on. He'd never have had time to learn how to do it while he was married and fulfilling family obligations out in the suburbs seven days a week. For Guy, it came as a revelation that he could pursue an enthusiasm of his very own; it beat spending all of his spare time looking after the house, the yard, and the needs of others.

MAKING FRIENDS THROUGH PLAY

Doing things you enjoy is also an excellent way to find people you enjoy spending time with. By exploring new interests, you'll find yourself making or enhancing friendships with people who share those interests.

Now's the time to call that friend or acquaintance who once invited you to play bridge, or who expressed an interest in going to a concert together or in playing a little tennis or golf. You don't need to feel as if you're making a big personal commitment, either. The commitment is no more binding than an agreement to get together once. If you enjoy the experience, you can repeat it sometime—or not, as the case may be.

By playing cards with X on Monday, attending a concert with Y on Thursday, or going for dinner with Z on Saturday, you can do some things you enjoy while building a social life. You can also spread yourself around among different friends, which is good for both you and them. You get the benefits of variety in the company you keep and the things you choose to do, while not depending too much on any one person.

Sometimes you have to experiment to find out which activities you enjoy most. You may not know if you like certain pastimes until you try them. If you don't enjoy something, you can always discard it and try something else. For example, I gave up golf after a few pathetic attempts—but the bridge group I formed one week after my separation is still going strong to this day, eleven years later.

Remember Linda from Chapter 2? She was the patient whose husband, Stan, moved out on her without warning after seven years. Linda actually recovered from the breakup more quickly than Stan, because she grieved over the death of the relationship, then got on with building her new life. She took to heart my suggestion to make time for herself and have some fun. With Stan gone, one of her kids off to college and the other out working, Linda had time on her hands for the first time in twenty years. She couldn't fill it all up with working (she was a senior nurse), so she started doing things she'd often wanted to do, but had put off for one reason or another.

Linda called up friends she hadn't had time for during the years with Stan. She arranged to go see a movie with them, or to have dinner on a Saturday night. She was a big fan of the local football team, so she got involved in the activities of the team's booster club. She spent a weekend with an old girlfriend who lived in another town, renewing an important friendship from years ago in nursing school.

Linda began to feel there were a lot of advantages to her new life; as did Grace, the mother of three we met in the last chapter, who held down two jobs because her husband was so delinquent with his support payments.

A year earlier, Grace had been literally in despair over her situation. She'd worried herself sick over her money problems (she was on the verge of personal bankruptcy) and her children's future, facing the prospect of having to move with her kids into the basement of her successful brother's suburban home. She felt humiliated: desperate, hopeless, practically suicidal.

Ultimately, Grace saw that living with her brother and his family just wouldn't work out. She was determined to pull herself out of the hole rather than throw herself on her brother's mercy. That was when she got the second job—a part-time position teaching night school—in addition to her daytime teaching job. Her two older children, girls aged sixteen and fourteen, took jobs after school to cover their clothing and entertainment expenses, and Grace applied to a local government agency that would enforce her separation agreement and help her recover the support money due from her ex-husband.

Gradually, her picture began to brighten. Not only did Grace manage to support her family financially, but her faith in herself as a capable, competent adult rose enormously. She even enrolled as a mature student in some university courses—although how she found the time and energy, I never quite understood.

This patient became a marvel of self-help and self-reliance. But one thing was missing from her life: the chance to have fun. Woman does not live by bread alone.

After eighteen months of keeping her nose to the grindstone, Grace allowed herself to take a weekend off to attend her high school reunion. First, however, she had to psyche herself up for it. She was fearful about what her old schoolmates would say about her—her divorce, her economic status, even her weight. She was convinced she'd become awfully fat (although she didn't look it to me).

But when she steeled herself to buy a new dress for the reunion—her first new dress in two years—Grace was astonished to find that she fit into a size eight right off the rack. Maybe she wasn't as fat as she'd thought! She had her hair done, stepped into her nifty new dress, and attended the reunion with some trepidation, not knowing what to expect—and had the best time, and the first fun, she'd enjoyed in years. She ended up renewing some friendships from her school days and agreeing to get together more often with her old friends from now on.

This patient was a real success story: a classic case of someone who learned, through hard experience, to be responsible to and for herself. Everything began coming together for Grace when she started caring about herself as a person. After learning to do that, she discovered other people respected and cared about her too.

CAROL'S STORY

First, a personal note: When I was separated, I couldn't find bedroom furniture that suited me. I wanted a queen-size bed, with large adjoining sidetables that had lots of room for lamps and books and magazines and stuff. In the end, I found a man who would build the furniture to my specifications. I was enormously pleased with the result, and surprised at how satisfying it could be to take control of my physical environment.

Similarly, a twice-divorced patient of mine found himself decorating his new one-bedroom apartment; he realized with amazement that it was the only time he'd ever designed his own living space in all of his fifty-six years. "You know, this is the first time I've had a place to myself," he marveled. In college, he'd lived in the men's dorm, then shared a house with roommates; he'd married immediately after graduation, then remarried, moving directly from his first wife to his second. So he'd always relied on other people—usually women—to provide the interior decor of the home. He'd never had to decide for himself which kind of sofa he liked best, or which style of drapes, or which colors. Now he was finding it tremendously satisfying to define and exercise his personal tastes.

This isn't an exclusively male experience. After being separated for eight months, Carol, too, found herself with the novel responsibility of taking charge of her own living space. All during college, she'd lived at home with her parents; immediately afterward, she'd married Richard and moved East. And since Richard had held such pronounced opinions on everything, which she'd imagined were far superior to hers, she'd never taken much initiative in decorating the homes in which they'd lived.

Eight months after Richard moved out of the matrimonial home, he and Carol agreed it would make financial sense for both of them to sell it. So Carol had a decision to make: whether to rent an apartment, buy a condominium with her share of the house proceeds, or buy another house. She wasn't sure which option was right for her. Then a small house she'd always admired came up for sale in the neighborhood; she went to look at it and just loved it. It was exactly what she wanted, so she made an offer and it was accepted. The house was hers.

Of course, before she moved, Carol and Richard had to divvy

up the contents of the matrimonial home. Previously, she'd have felt unequal in such a negotiation, completely intimidated by Richard. Not this time! They had some dandy arguments about who should get what, but by now Carol had developed enough self-confidence to hold her ground and refuse to be browbeaten. She used the kind of calm, rational arguments that were formerly Richard's specialty—to the point where he could hardly disagree with her, and he actually became unusually accommodating. As a result, they drew up a detailed agreement about the division of assets, thus reducing both their legal expenses considerably.

Carol was as excited as a schoolgirl about moving into her new home. One of its nicest features was a sunken living room with a stone fireplace; she'd always pictured herself curling up on the sofa in front of the fire with a good book. But now she had no sofa—in fact she had no living room furniture at all. She'd traded it to Richard for the paintings, the ceramic collection, and the sound system, all of which held more personal value for her.

Carol wanted her new living room to look just right. But since she was unsure how to go about decorating it, she asked friends to recommend some good interior decorators. (She could afford this service, since she'd received a bigger share of the house profits in return for allowing Richard to keep the cottage.) In the end, Carol met with three different decorators before she found one whose ideas pleased her. She didn't just accept the recommendations of the first one she talked to. She was learning to trust her own judgment, to do things her way.

Not everyone has Carol's material advantages and can afford to hire a decorator. Yet the principle remains the same, whatever your circumstances. Your living quarters are important. After all, they're an extension of you, and you're important. There's something highly symbolic—and satisfying—about being able to take charge of shaping your own environment.

LIVING FOR TODAY, AND FIVE YEARS FROM TODAY

When you're caught up in the swirling concerns of the moment, excited about all the new things that are happening for you, it's easy to lose sight of the overall direction your life is taking. This can be such a momentous time of evolution and *becoming* that your perspective on the future can be overwhelmed. Yet we all need to have some sort of long-term view of where we're going.

This sounds like a contradiction of what I've just said about having fun, but it isn't really. While you need to live life as it comes and take pleasure in the present, at the same time, you need to keep an eye on the direction you're heading in. Life is an evolving, developmental process; the decisions we make today affect where we'll be five years from today. As someone responsible to and for yourself, you're responsible for who you are now, and who you're becoming as well.

One of the first questions I ask new patients is, "Where would you like to be five years from now?" People hesitate to answer—because either they're not sure, or they don't want to appear "selfish" or "pretentious." But the next time they come in to see me, they've usually thought about it, and the question doesn't seem so outlandish after all. They find that answering it helps them arrive at a clearer sense of who they are and what they want to be.

I'm not suggesting that you set rigid or ambitious goals by which to judge yourself. I'm only saying that, in taking responsibility for yourself today, you're taking responsibility for setting a direction for the future. Of course, you can change or modify that direction if you so desire. Five years from today is never a fixed, unalterable point, but a destination that moves forward a notch every day.

Also, while this time can be a period of euphoria, it's unlikely you'll feel euphoric all of the time. Indeed, you may still occasionally experience the return of the old sadness from your grieving period, expressed as a bout of loneliness or depression, when you wonder why you're bothering to do the things you're doing. What's the use, you may wonder.

At times like that, it's valuable to have a conscious direction for your life. This direction helps you to recall where you're going and why. It strengthens your resolve to get there, because you can look back and see how far you've come in overcoming grief and sadness, in feeling better about your life. If you've come this far already, in such a relatively short span of time, just imagine how much further you'll progress in the months and years ahead!

BILL'S STORY

For someone who'd lived a dutiful life, always seeing himself as a husband and father, a caretaker and provider, and similarly seeing others in terms of roles, Bill showed a remarkable capacity for evolving into an authentic person in his own right. Once he started caring about himself as a person, he began to discover what was interesting and unique about other people, too.

In earlier chapters, we saw Bill learning to relax with his children and getting his mind off his carpet business for a while. But he still needed to learn how to do things just for himself—just for fun. He needed to find more constructive ways to unwind than holing up in his apartment with a six-pack, or drinking a whole bottle of wine with dinner. Bill also needed friends, people he could enjoy spending time with outside of work. These two things—activities and friends—could provide him with the stimulation and balance he needed. They could offer new outlets for his energies besides the traditional ones of family and job.

One day, Bill came to see me after I'd been away for several weeks on my summer vacation (psychiatrists need to have fun too). Life had been going better, Bill told me—a lot better. He'd been seeing more of his kids and slowing down some at work. Gradually, he'd discover that his store manager, Mario, was a very capable, competent employee, so he'd given Mario progressively more responsibility and raised his salary, which allowed Bill to back off a bit from the day-to-day operations.

He also found Mario to be a pretty nice guy, Bill remarked, as if surprised to realize that nice guys actually exist in the business world. Not only that, Mario belonged to a golf club. Now, Bill had to admit he wasn't much of a golfer—he'd never done much more than hack a ball around a course a couple of times a year, whenever one of his suppliers held golf afternoons, which were really just excuses to get a little drunk and swap outrageous stories. But when Mario invited him to help make a foursome at the club, Bill thought it might be worth a try. To limber up his swing, he took Jordan and Lisa with him to a driving range, where they had fun driving a couple of buckets of balls. Bill hoped the practice would save him from being too embarrassed on the tee.

"You know, Doc, I wasn't as bad out there as I thought I'd be," he said. "No worse than one of the other guys, anyway. We played all eighteen holes, and it was the best time I've had in years. They're a great bunch of guys. Nobody worried about anything, except how miserable their shots were."

With a note of wonderment, Bill remarked that neither of Mario's friends was "even in the trade." One was an insurance agent; the other ran a restaurant. The latter was quite a cosmopolitan guy, who'd trained as a chef in Switzerland and had worked in Italy. Now he had his own restaurant downtown and seemed to be making a go of it.

After the golf game, the four men drank one beer each back in the clubhouse. They compared notes about the course, argued over who had made the worst shot, and had a few laughs. Bill felt so good about the experience, so relaxed after the sunshine and exercise, he told Mario that if he ever needed a fourth again, to please count him in. And as it turned out, one of the regulars was absent for both of the next two weekends, so Bill got to play twice more.

"I'm practically a regular now," he told me with quiet pride. "In fact, I've made my mind up—I'm going to join that club. Mario and the others have agreed to be my sponsors. There's a whole bunch of nice people there. And in the winter it's a curling club, and I'm going to get involved in that, too."

This was a real change for Bill, a new direction in his life. He'd never seemed to have much capacity for fun before. But now he was growing enthusiastic, expansive—all because of a pleasurable activity that he was pursuing just for himself. His kids weren't involved; he didn't have to take care of anybody; he could just be himself, have some fun, and make friends.

Previously, Bill had always tried to meet his social needs through his family and his large group of relatives. Now he was into a whole new world. Tony, the chef, had even invited the golf partners to his restaurant for dinner the next week. He'd selected a special menu for them, and they all had to promise not to talk shop—especially Bill and Mario.

"I never thought I'd say this, but I can let my hair down with those guys. Doesn't even seem to bother them that I'm separated. And I just feel so relaxed with them, especially after a game of golf, that I don't need to drink, not nearly as much as I used to."

By finding a more constructive way to spend leisure time, Bill had less need to unwind with alcohol. This harks back to what we discussed in Chapter 3 about the pitfalls of excess and the need to strike a balance in life through different interests and activities. At last Bill was moving away from some of his pitfalls.

"And—oh yeah," he said as a parting thought, "I almost forgot. When we were at the clubhouse last time, Tony introduced me to this interesting woman: Charlene. She's in computer sales. Sold Tony the billing system for his restaurant. Anyway, she and I talked and we sort of hit it off. Here's her card. I don't know, I'm even thinking of maybe asking her out sometime. . . ."

Chapter Eight

Dating, and Other Terrors

As we've seen, sooner or later you're going to want to restart your social life. By "social life," I mean not only seeing family and old, familiar friends, as important as they are, but also getting out and meeting new people. You'll want to have some adventures, take a risk on the unexpected—even date!

For many of us, reentering the social scene can be extremely daunting. We've spent so much of our adult lives as part of a couple that we're not sure how to relate to others as a single person. The prospect of getting to know complete strangers from scratch seems threatening, fraught with anxiety. It's so much easier to sit at home watching *Roseanne* or reruns of *Cheers*. At least the television doesn't ask prying questions that you're too self-conscious or embarrassed to answer.

Sometimes this problem can look pretty overwhelming. Your old friends aren't as available as they once seemed. Many of them are involved in marriages or close relationships, doing activities with other couples. You may feel reluctant to "impose" on them, unsure how you fit into their scheme of things. So those friend-ships don't work as well for you as they used to. Besides, you admit to yourself, you didn't really enjoy some of those "couple" activi-ties all that much anyway!

The question is, what are you going to do for a social life now? Because you do get lonely sometimes. You do long for compan-ionship, for shared experiences, for fun. Yet it's such a couples' world out there that you feel shut out. Couples go to movies to-gether, to nice restaurants, to parties; everybody else is in cou-ples—or so it seems. There's practically nobody in the universe who's single like you.

My male patients say, "There's supposed to be lots of single women out there, Doctor—but damned if I know where to find them." Female patients tell me, "There are single men out there, all right, but they're all rejects. The good ones are taken."

Now, can that really be true? In my profession, I meet plenty of single adults of both sexes, and most of them are very fine and interesting people. I suppose that if I wanted to change jobs, I could always set up a singles introduction service and I'd get plenty of business. In fact, some people may feel tempted to try such a service, in order to meet interesting people of the opposite sex. But let's look at some other ideas that are likely to be far more productive and satisfying in the long run. We'll start by picking up Carol's story at the point where she joined the tennis club.

CAROL'S STORY

In Chapter 4, we saw how pleased Carol felt about her decision to sign up for tennis club membership. For her, given her shortage of self-confidence, it was a real breakthrough. It meant she was starting to take steps, however basic, to meet her own adult needs. And six months after joining the club, Carol was even more pleased. Her experiences there had turned out to be enormously positive.

Remember how she'd decided to attend a social evening at the club on the Saturday after she joined? It had cost her a huge effort to follow through on that plan and actually show up. "I took abso-lutely forever to get ready," she told me. "I could hardly believe

I was really going to do this—attend a buffet dinner and dance where I didn't know a soul."

She arrived at the club late, squeezed her car into the last remaining space at the far end of the parking lot, and went inside. She could hear the sounds of music, laughter, and clinking glasses coming from the dance upstairs. She stood there at the foot of the staircase, her stomach in knots, wondering how she was ever going to make her entrance. In her mind, this truly represented a "coming out." Who else would be there? What should she say? What should she do? How would she even explain her presence? Carol was tempted to turn and run—after all, she was alone, nobody would see her.

But she'd solemnly promised herself she was going to attend: It had been ages since she'd tried anything new, outside of working and seeing colleagues at the office; she had to start somewhere. Besides, when she'd signed up to join the club, she'd promised Harry, the president, that she'd come to the dance. She steeled herself to march up the staircase and into the lions' den.

"When I got up there, I couldn't believe my luck," Carol said. "There was Harry at the top of the stairs, waiting to greet me. It was like seeing an old friend."

Harry was wonderful. He escorted Carol inside, got her a drink, and introduced her to his girlfriend, May. Harry and May were the kind of warm, chatty, outgoing people who make marvelous hosts. They encouraged Carol to feel so at home, it was as if she'd known them forever. Over the course of the evening, they introduced her to more people than she could remember meeting in the whole of the previous year. She danced with five different men and stayed far later than she'd expected to.

To her surprise, Carol also signed up that night to play in a mixed-doubles tournament the following weekend. She felt she wasn't really ready for tournament play, but she entered a novice category where she wouldn't be too outclassed. Besides, she didn't have to worry about all the critical things Richard would say if he'd been there. She'd be paired with a nice young man, who seemed terribly pleased just to have found a partner.

Over the ensuing months, Carol took weekly tennis lessons, which gradually improved her game, although she happily admitted she'd never be Chris Evert or Steffi Graf. She enjoyed playing tennis, and felt good about becoming more fit, even a little slim-mer. What she really valued most about the club was that it served her as a base for a new and much-expanded social life.

Carol spent an evening or two at the club every week, and often a whole day on the weekends. She not only took lessons and played in tournaments, but she enjoyed all the social functions as well. This was a truly fundamental change in her life. For a woman in her late thirties with no children, Carol found the ten-nis club better than a dating service or a singles bar for meeting people of both sexes with whom she had things in common.

Soon, a variety of members had become her friends; after six months, she was asked to run for membership secretary of the club executive board. She agreed, and was elected unanimously. People had come to like and value Carol as an intelligent, capable person. On the executive board, she felt needed and appreciated; the old executive board had allowed the membership to run down, and her managerial and personnel skills were invaluable in finding new members to boost the club's revenues back up again.

The tennis club came to represent community to Carol. It served her well in that capacity for the next couple of years, pro-viding her not only with friends, but with growth in her self-es-teem from knowing that she'd had the courage to take a risk that paid off. As we'll see in the next chapter, the experience eventually led to a relationship that would become extremely important to her life. But for the time being, the club was a source of chums for Carol to play with.

It was this success in finding chums to play with, more than anything else, that helped Carol learn to live successfully on her own again. In the process, she sidestepped one of the biggest pit-falls of all: looking for the elusive Mr. Right.

WHY MR. (OR MS.) RIGHT IS ALL WRONG

I once had a patient who gave me a doll of stuffed fabric. It was a wonderfully gross-looking character, with googly crossed eyes, blackened teeth, hair askew every which way, and horribly loud clothes. I liked it so much that I propped it on a stool in the corner of my office, where it could leer across at my patients. The name tag pinned to its oversized lapel said "Mr. Right."

My stuffed companion was ideal for getting across a great truth for our times: Looking for Mr. or Ms. So-called Right is all wrong. I've seen too many people who leap prematurely into the arms of someone they've mistakenly thought was their "savior"; or who forever seek the "perfect" mate, only to find that every prospective candidate has fatal flaws that disqualify him or her.

Looking for Mr. or Ms. Right just doesn't work. Why? Because we're really looking, more often than not, for an idealized mother or father—someone who's going to be just perfect for us and fulfill our every need. That fact is, no such person exists. You had your last perfect relationship when you were two months old and were being nursed by your mom. She satisfied all your simple, basic, two-month-old needs and made the world perfect for you. It's time to acknowledge that no relationship ever will do that again.

In your single state, you may still be coping with the nagging, gnawing feeling that you're not a "whole" person. "I'll only feel like a whole person," you tell yourself, "when I can find someone to complete me."

That's a classic formulation of the adolescent marriage bargain, "You take care of me, I'll take care of you." It also represents a huge danger for a grown-up wishing to embark on adult relationships. It can lead you straight to Mr. or Ms. Wrong.

GETTING TO KNOW YOU

One reason why you don't feel like a whole person is that you haven't yet discovered enough about yourself. How do you do that? By pursuing your own interests, by exploring things that appeal to you. That way, you learn more about who you are. It's a discovery well worth making. In the process, you'll meet people who share your interests. Some of them will be women; some, men. They're all potential chums to play with.

Which activities you pursue depend entirely on you. What do you like doing? Some interests, like bridge or team sports, are clearly group activities requiring other people. Other pastimes are more solitary in nature; you're accustomed to enjoying them alone, whether it's yoga, reading, sketching, or fishing.

But—you can also do yoga by attending a class at the local "Y" or community center. You can join a reading circle, where members meet every month at somebody's home to discuss the latest bestseller. You can take a drawing course with professional instructors and live models. You can even sign up with a rod-and-reel club that offers wilderness fishing trips. Indeed, many interest groups, from sporting clubs to professional associations to museum groups, provide their members with good deals on package tours.

In other words, there's no need to be alone when enjoying your favorite interests. While doing these things, you can meet men and women with similar tastes. They're people first, people who share something in common with you. If you pursue two or three interests in this fashion, you're sure to meet a whole bunch of people, of whom one, or two, or even more could become your friends—never mind whether or not they're Mr. or Mrs. Right.

By pursuing your interests, and making friends in the process, you're learning about who *you* are. Friends act as mirrors: They help you to find out what you look like, in a manner of speaking.

Think of a world where there were no mirrors or other reflecting surfaces such as water or glass—how would you know what you look like? Similarly, we need reflecting surfaces in the form of friends to help us learn about who we are. The reflecting surfaces don't *determine* who we are, they can only offer an approximate likeness. And since there are no such things as perfect mirrors, some of the flaws they reflect are actually within the mirrors themselves. But, allowing for these distortions, we can get a pretty fair idea of who and what we are through our interactions with others and the way others respond to us. That's one good reason why we need friendships.

Note, however, that these mirrors don't dictate our behavior to us. They don't tell us what we *should* be. You don't use them to learn how to dress the way *he* likes—or to behave the way *she* wants—in place of being yourself.

Another good reason for having friendships is that they help meet that fundamental adult need, discussed earlier, to be cared about as a person. Meeting this need begins within, by caring about ourselves as persons; through relationships, we extend and deepen our ability to meet this need. The closer the relationship, the more likely that this need will get met.

So now is the time to discover more about yourself by pursuing the things you like, in the company of people who can become mirrors that tell you still more about what you like—in yourself and others. This is an extremely different process from the concept of needing to "complete" yourself through that one "perfect" person.

REMAKING COMMUNITY

As you find new chums to play with, you also remake your sense of community. Once, your community was shaped largely by your involvements with work, family, and possibly, religion, and it included the people you met through those institutions. Now you're establishing new and more personal connections with others—independent of institutions. And if you meet twenty, or fifty, or a hundred people by pursuing your various interests, maybe one of them will become your personal friend. Maybe two will; maybe five.

Among all the people you meet in this way, how do you identify which ones you want to be friends with? It's simple. You talk to them.

Let's say you've always wanted to learn Spanish. So you enroll in an evening course offered by a local college, school board, or "Y". Before the class begins, during coffee break, or after class, you chat with different people to see what they're like—nothing heavy, just small talk about the class or the weather or irregular verbs.

It will quickly become obvious to you which people you're comfortable talking with, and which ones are comfortable talking with you. Don't rush it—just take opportunities to socialize as they come along. Eventually, it will feel appropriate to suggest going out for coffee after class, or maybe the other person will suggest it. It's not a big deal, or a huge investment of time or money: You're just going out for coffee with someone.

This way, little by little, you'll learn about the other people, and they'll learn about you. Maybe you'll conclude that there's no one in the class you want to spend time with, and that's fine: At least you're learning Spanish, which is why you went there in the first place! So you're not wasting your time. But if you do make a friend or two, it's an additional benefit of pursuing an interest that's important to you.

For the Spanish class, substitute your church group, a camera club, a single parents' organization, a women's group: whatever your particular interest happens to be at the moment. The friendships you make through these activities may or may not last beyond the activities themselves. And that's okay too—these people don't have to become friends for life (which is just another way of describing Mr. or Ms. Right).

No, you're simply looking for people to play with. You're saying, I don't want to be lonely, so I'll pursue my interests in the company of other adults. Remember, you may be on your own, but you don't have to be alone. There's nothing requiring that you have to *like* being alone, much less that you have to like feeling lonely.

Let's extend this approach of remaking your community. At the Spanish class, there may be someone in the same situation as you—a recently separated person; a single mother or father. You get to talking, and find you both have that in common. So one of you tells the other about a discussion group for divorced people, a good day-care center, or a single parents' organization; or you offer to do babysitting for each other, or offer to go out to a movie together on Friday night. And there you go, another chum to play with. Now, if that other person is of the opposite sex, you can call it a "date," if you like—but basically, you're still just going to see a movie.

Another advantage of joining interest groups is that they sometimes offer travel opportunities. Traveling alone can be difficult, especially for women. Many people find the solution in group tours. Even then, however, you usually end up sharing accommodations with someone you don't know—unless you're prepared to pay an additional premium for a single room, since most prices are based on double occupancy.

One way to get around this problem is to take a trip organized by a group you belong to: an art gallery association, ski club, alumni association, professional union, and so on. This gives you the advantage of knowing, and having some things in common with, the people with whom you're traveling. As a result, you're more likely to find someone with whom you want to share a room. It's always nice to know who is in the bed next to yours.

These tours usually involve going first to a lecture series or slide presentation, which allows you to chat with other members and get to know potential roommates before committing yourself to sharing a hotel room on a Mexican beach or a Greek island.

THE SINGLES SCENE

There are various social situations especially designed for single people, ranging from discussion and self-help groups, singles gourmet cooking classes, and singles dances, to the singles-bar scene, with its "meat-market" connotations. Which of these you choose depends on what you're comfortable with. How successful the experience is depends on the attitudes you bring to it. The main thing is not to entertain grandiose expectations and demands. Keeping your expectations realistic takes a lot of the pressure and fear out of getting to know other single adults.

If you go to a party, dance, singles bar, or any other social situation looking for Mr. or Ms. Right, then you're heading for frustration and disappointment. Even if you think "tonight's the night" you're going to meet someone wonderfully attractive and irresistible, if only for this one night, you're still looking for trouble. The chances are that romantic character won't show up—he or she must be in Boise tonight—and you'll end the evening alone, dejected and depressed, a victim of your own fantasy.

But if you go out with the expectation that you're going to meet a few people and talk to them, maybe have a drink or two, dance a little, and then go home, it's unlikely you'll be disappointed. You'll be satisfied with the experience: In all probability there *will* be people to talk to or dance with, and in all probability it will be fun—at least a little. And you won't be setting yourself up for a big fall.

In the last chapter, we talked about the advantages of having a home away from home, a friendly restaurant, café, or watering hole where you can become one of the regulars. My patient Heather found such a place, a singles bar and restaurant near her apartment, where she could drop in whenever she felt like having some company. Heather wasn't looking for romance or for casual sex, but she invariably found a few gregarious people of both sexes to talk to. They gave her the amusement and companionship she was looking for right then. Afterward, she always went home alone.

Heather made a rule for herself, which she followed religiously: never to date or take home any of the men she met at her favorite spot. The reason was that she wanted to remain free to go there whenever she pleased, without the pressure of becoming "the date" of one of the other regulars. Heather wanted her own space, and made sure she got it.

Claudine, on the other hand, tried the singles-bar scene before she was ready to handle it. After her divorce, aside from caring for her house and two young children, Claudine withdrew from people almost entirely. She used her responsibilities as a single mother as an excuse to stay home and hide her crippling anxiety from the world. After eight months of brooding over her lost marriage and uncertain future, Claudine realized she was actually desperate for a little adult company, so she allowed a well-meaning female friend, also separated, to talk her into going to a bar/restaurant favored by singles.

Claudine sat at a corner table with her friend, nervously sipping a margarita in the semidarkness. And whenever a guy wandered over to make conversation with her, she froze up, fending off their inoffensive questions with curt, one-word responses.

"What exactly do you do?" one asked. "Nothing," she replied. "Ever been here before?" "No."

"Where do you go for fun?" "Nowhere."

The whole experience was excruciating for Claudine, a real travesty. Unfortunately, it put her off socializing for several more months. The singles-bar scene just wasn't right for the shy, anxious person that she was right then.

In fact, other social activities would have suited Claudine's reentry into the world much better: a women's self-help group, a single-parents' organization, an interesting course, a church group. Taking a morning exercise class, or volunteering at a hospital or senior citizens' home while her kids were at school, would have gotten her out of the house, and given her the beginnings of a life outside of home and family. These kinds of activities would also have brought her into contact with other sympathetic adults, contact she needed badly. She might have made a friend or two: a bonus to an activity that was already worth doing in itself.

My patient Gary, a thirty-something-ish lawyer, had a different kind of experience with singles bars. Gary had been divorced for over a year and had arranged for shared custody of five-year-old Todd, who lived with him on alternate weeks. During the weeks when he didn't have Todd, Gary would drop by his local hangout, Whispers, on a Wednesday or Thursday evening. His usual pattern was to stay late at the office catching up on his paperwork on those evenings, then leave around seven-thirty and drive to Whispers for a light dinner and a glass of wine. He'd kibbitz with a few of the regulars he'd come to know, maybe have another drink, then get home by eleven so he wouldn't be tired at work the next day. He always had a pleasant time.

Gary didn't try to pick up women at Whispers. He did date one woman he met there, an accountant with a public-relations firm, who accompanied him to a movie and a company barbecue. They didn't get into a heavy romantic relationship, but enjoyed each other's company, and left it at that.

At least once a week, Gary had a nice evening out, socializing in familiar and comfortable surroundings. Other patrons might have gone there to hustle women or drink themselves blind; Gary preferred a regular weekly occasion where he could relax, gossip, and laugh a little—rather like dropping in on a perpetual cocktail party. For Gary, Whispers fulfilled the function of the Spanish class, or Carol's tennis club. He found it was more fun to live out *Cheers* than stay home and watch it on television.

DATING GAMES

Just about every separated or divorced person feels like a sixteen-year-old when they start dating again. As we get ready for the Big Night, we feel exactly as we did when we were teenagers dressing for the prom—breathless, sweating, giddy, terrified. And that's the trouble. Heaven knows, we're not kids anymore.

Let me tell my personal anecdote. Two months after I separated, my friend Nancy tried to fix me up with a friend of hers.

I'd never met the woman before; it would be a blind date.

I felt extremely anxious about the whole thing. But I wanted to be a good sport, so I agreed to call the woman in question to make arrangements to meet, and also to get to know her a bit over the phone. Suddenly, a lot of silly questions invaded my mind, questions I hadn't asked myself since I was sixteen: How tall is she? Nancy says she's "nice"—does that really mean she's ugly? Will she like me? What'll we talk about? She's recently separated too—will we have anything to discuss besides our misery? Do I really want to know about her troubles with her rat of an ex-husband? And why did he leave her in the first place? Was it because she's such a loser?

No doubt the poor woman was wondering the same things about me. And then there we were, talking on the phone. It was bizarre. Haltingly, fumblingly, we made our introductions—and before we knew it, we discovered there was no mutually convenient time for us to meet. Sweating with relief, I hung up. A week or so later, I tried again; again, no luck. And guess what? We never did get together for that blind date—and I never got answers to my silly questions. I could only shake my head over the way my old teenage angst had come flooding back. I'd assumed I'd put it all behind me twenty years earlier.

I'm sure ninety percent of us experience some variation of this story when we start dating again. After all, our memories and expectations of dating originated in adolescence. We sometimes forget that we're not teenagers anymore, and don't need to burden ourselves with those old anxieties based on teenage ignorance, insecurity, and fantasy. We forget we can just relax and let the experience unfold. Whatever happens, you can handle it—you're an autonomous adult now. Maybe a teenager couldn't handle it, but you can.

Going out on a dinner date? Well, you've been out for dinner with other adults many times—it's no big deal. Going to a movie with someone? You've been to movies before, too. You'll go to the theater, and before and after the show you'll talk, and you'll either make friends or you won't. There isn't a whole lot at stake.

So what's riding on a date? Nothing. But what do you *think* is riding on it? Everything: your self-esteem; your identity as a sexual being—your whole romantic future!

In reality, what you probably stand to get out of the experience is a pleasant evening. Of course, the other person may turn out to be an obnoxious bore, in which case you'll have a terrible evening. But that's not your responsibility. Either way, the most you're risking is three or four hours of your time. If the date turns out to be a disaster, then maybe at least the dinner was good, or the movie entertaining. You haven't really lost anything.

It's amazing how difficult it can be to accept this. The old teenage angst dies hard. And that's too bad, because it can tie us up in knots—often over someone we don't even know that well, or care about that much.

The adolescent games we play around dating happen mostly in our own heads. They have more to do with teenage romantic dreams of "Make my life complete" than with any real relationship.

TRUDY AND THE VAN MAN

These games were taken to an extreme by Trudy, a thirty-four-year-old, never-married sales manager who loved to travel. When abroad, Trudy was fearless and intrepid, often volunteering to lead tour groups from her hometown on hiking holidays in the Yucatan or the Himalayas. She even traveled alone on a bus tour of South America.

When Trudy was home, she acted very differently. She'd begun one hot relationship with a guy while paddling up the Amazon, sleeping in hammocks in the jungle among dangerous snakes and reptiles. On their return, she found she couldn't sustain this affair—she couldn't handle his many imperfections. He wasn't Mr. Right after all.

Trudy met another interesting man at her athletic club. They enjoyed playing squash together, and she was an even match for him on the court. As she grew interested in him, Trudy badly wanted to go out on a date with him, but he never asked her out.

One evening, they attended the same party at the club. Drink in hand, Trudy sidled over to the object of her desire, who was chatting with someone else, his back to her. Trudy told herself she'd give him exactly half an hour to notice her and come over to talk; if he didn't respond in the allotted time, she'd leave the party.

He didn't respond. She left. She felt crushed, devastated.

"If he was interested in me, he'd have come over and talked!" Trudy lamented to me. But, I reminded her, she hadn't explained the rules to him. How was he supposed to know how to play this game? She hadn't even said, "Hi, how are you?"

Over the next few months, Mr. Desirable got involved with someone else, leading Trudy to say, "I told you so." If she'd been more forthright about showing her interest in him, he might have gotten involved with her. But by reacting like a helpless teenager with a crush, Trudy undermined herself, setting herself up to be rejected. This was her biggest fear in the first place, and it turned into a self-fulfilling prophecy. She then felt even more rejected, which discouraged her from pursuing other relationships with men.

Sometimes it can be hard to remember that you really are a thirty-four-old adult and not a fifteen-year-old teenager. You need to remind yourself that you're capable and competent while at work, raising your kids, or being with your friends; you can be the same way in your dating relationships. You don't need to regress to being a wimpy adolescent with a hopeless crush, just because you're attracted to someone. What makes *them* so powerful anyway? You have a lot going for you, too.

Things turned out differently for Larry, a delivery-van driver for one of the big department store chains. But then, he started with the enormous advantage of not looking for Ms. Right under every rock.

At forty, Larry had gone through a reasonably amicable divorce from his wife of fourteen years. She had custody of their twelve-year-old daughter, while he had custody of nine-year-old Brent. Even after a year, Larry remained a little shaken by his marriage breakup: Wary of what could happen if he got too close to someone, he was in no big hurry to recouple. He still hadn't been out on a single date.

In his apartment building lived Jill, another single parent, who worked part-time doing telemarketing at home and whose two kids attended Brent's school. Jill's children were both a little younger than Brent, but they were close enough to him in age that they all got along. Larry paid Jill to provide after-school care for Brent until he got home from work, which varied a lot depending on the volume of deliveries he had to make. He was grateful there was someone in the building he could count on to back him up. It was a very satisfactory arrangement.

After a PTA meeting that they both attended, Larry and Jill got talking about the Christmas dance that the PTA was holding as a fundraiser. One of them said, "Gee, I'd like to go, but I don't really know anybody," and the other said, "Me too, I guess." Finally, they got around to agreeing that, well, maybe they could go together. Somehow it was understood that this wasn't really a date—just a practical solution, like their babysitting arrangement.

Larry and Jill went to the dance together and had a good time. Gradually they discovered they actually had more in common than they'd realized. They were both quite serious about education (both wished they were better educated), and about their children's social and emotional development; it was helpful to talk about the issues involved in single-parenting. They both enjoyed "improving" books, and swapping ideas they'd discovered in their reading. They took the kids bowling and out to movies; they ordered in pizza on Friday nights.

Several months passed in this way before Larry and Jill acknowledged they were "sort of" going out together—not just doing things out of convenience. Somewhere in the middle of all that, they became sexually intimate. Until then, the idea of admitting they were becoming emotionally involved was just too scary.

Eventually, little by little, they moved in together. And lived happily—if not ever after, at least until now.

The significance of this story lies in the fact that Larry and Jill didn't start out seeking another person to give meaning to their lives: Their lives already had meaning. The lack of expectations took the pressure off their relationship, which was allowed to grow naturally out of the functional, helpful things they did for each other. They were able to establish a solid relationship based on the realities of shared interests and personal compatibility, instead of weighing it down with inflated romantic expectations.

Both of them had felt so nervous about dating that they couldn't handle the idea of getting "romantic" so soon. Their relationship actually had a better chance of lasting because they took it slowly, learning to trust and respect each other. They could then risk intimacy, because both of them knew what the other was made of.

BILL'S STORY

Let's pick up Bill where we left him last time, just after meeting the computer salesperson, Charlene, at the golf club.

To his surprise, Charlene gave him a call shortly afterward to say her company was throwing a banquet, and she wondered if he'd like to go as her date. Bill was thoroughly taken aback. He was a pretty traditional guy, unused to having a woman act so assertively toward him. He wasn't sure how to handle the situation: He'd never been taken along by a woman to a social event as "her" man. Still, backed to the wall, he said yes.

But now he had a whole bunch of questions: "Who buys the drinks, me or her? Who am I going to talk to besides Charlene? What am I going to *say* to *her*? What's she expecting? Do we have anything in common?" On top of that, he realized, he'd have to be careful not to drink too much, because he liked Charlene and didn't want to blow his chances with her.

What a heavy trip for a first date! Couldn't they just go to a movie or something?

Bill came in to see me before the Big Event. He spilled out all his anxieties, all his agonized questions. He was afraid it would all be too much for him, and he hoped I could get him ready, as if he were a sprinter training for the Olympics.

Most of his questions were of the "What if?" variety, to which my answers were mostly, "So what?"

"What if I go down in her eyes when she discovers Marie kicked me out?"

"So what?"

"What if I can't hold my own with her computer colleagues?"

"So what?"

"What if she finds my business boring?"

"So what?"

Bill was concerned that Marie had always said he never knew anything but the carpet business. Well, I suggested, then this was his chance to learn something new. He could ask questions, keep his ears open. He didn't have to "blind them with science." Maybe he'd learn something that he could usefully apply to his own business.

I reminded him that he could draw on his experiences at the

golf club. There, he'd learned he could talk to people about something besides carpets—and he could do it again. This was just
another bunch of human beings he was about to meet, no big
deal. He could go and see what happens. What did he have to
lose?

"Well, Charlene."

"So what? You don't even *have* her to lose. And if it isn't the
greatest evening you've ever had, the world won't end. What's
really at stake?"

"There's a lot at stake, Doc. I'm going to find out if I can make
it with a woman after all."

"No, you're not. You're going to find out whether you and
Charlene can have a good time at a party. *She* seems to think you
will, or she wouldn't have invited you. She just wants to get to
know you."

"You think maybe she likes me?"

"Maybe. At least you'll get a good dinner out of it. You might
even meet some interesting folks. It'll be fun."

"So I suppose I'll just drive her home afterward and that'll be
that."

"Right. For the moment anyway."

"But if we have a good time, maybe we'll go out again."

"Of course."

"But what if I can't get it up?"

"Hey, wait a minute, fella—she's only asked you to dinner!"

As a lot of people do (and not only men), Bill was immediately
making the mental leap from getting invited out to getting married. He was forgetting there are a few steps in between—especially
for experienced adults who ought to know better.

Bill was also on the verge of jumping from "What if I can't get
it up?" to "What if she doesn't consider me a good provider?" Yet
neither question had yet become an issue. All he was doing was
loading pressure onto himself and Charlene, before they'd had a
chance to find out if they even liked each other.

Until now, Bill had been taking things one step at a time. He'd
gone into golfing for the right reasons—not to find Ms. Right, but
to enjoy himself by playing a game he liked with some other people he liked. So far, so good. It was only when one of those people
turned out to be of the opposite sex that his expectations became

unrealistic, and he started putting all this adolescent pressure on himself. If only he could have seen Charlene as just one of the boys! As it was, he was so fussed that he was practically ready to call the whole date off.

It was time for Bill to apply the lessons he'd learned during the previous few months. To meet his own adult needs, not someone else's. To be himself. To get out into the world and be appreciated as a person in his own right. To relax and have a little fun.

How Marie and Charlene saw Bill wasn't the issue for him. They didn't determine who he was, or what he was worth. His image didn't originate in the mirror, but in himself.

After we talked this over, Bill eased the pressure off himself and agreed to give dating Charlene a try. If anything further developed out of the relationship, that was for another day. For now, he'd get from the experience what *he* needed.

Stage Four
Getting Comfortable

The final stage of learning to be on your own again usually occupies Year Three. By now, you're more comfortable being yourself—so much that you can also be comfortable in closer, more involved, more intimate relationships. Perhaps even a *most* intimate relationship, resulting in recoupling.

The model for an adult intimate relationship is a friendship with someone you care deeply about. Such a relationship is based on respect, trust, caring *about*. You don't try to change your friends into your image of what they should be, but allow them the space to be themselves. It's the same with adult intimacy.

Your aim doesn't have to be recoupling. Adult intimacy doesn't automatically mean you cohabit with someone. And it doesn't have to be exclusive, or even necessarily sexual. Your aim is to continue being a person on your own terms.

Even in an exclusive, monogamous commitment, you're still on your own in a very real sense—responsible to and for yourself. When you've decided to share your life with someone else, it is on terms that are comfortable for you as an autonomous adult.

Chapter Nine

Intimacy Again

Did you think I'd *never* get around to sex?

Of course, there's a lot more to intimacy than sex. Intimacy is about closeness and caring, trust and respect: a whole complex of shared feelings and emotional give-and-take. But sex does have a way of becoming part of an intimate relationship—and a pretty important part, at that. We're physical creatures, and sex can be the physical expression of the intellectual, emotional, or spiritual intimacy between two people. Sexual sharing can lead to the deeper emotional sharing sometimes known as love.

On the other hand, sometimes sex is just sex, and nothing more. This chapter is therefore about intimacy in both the basic physical sense, and the broader emotional sense of individuals who have chosen to share something more than their bodies.

Needless to say, intimacy is very big subject. It deserves a whole book to itself, maybe a whole library. In this book, intimacy occupies the territory between the subject of the last chapter—socializing and dating—and the subject of the next chapter—facing the question of whether you want to become part of an exclusive couple again.

It's certainly possible to become intimate with someone, sexually or otherwise, without making a binding commitment to recouple. One of the great advantages of reaching this stage in your life is that you're free to make that choice for yourself.

Wait a minute, you say, I've always been free to choose.

Well, yes and no. In this chapter, we'll look at the crucial differences between intimacy in adult relationships, such as those you enter into now, and intimacy in your earlier relationships, which were basically adolescent in nature. There's a world of difference.

To begin, let's pick up the story of Emma, the real-estate agent we met in Chapter 7, who was fond of bicycling and wicker furniture. Emma got involved in two different relationships, illustrating the different faces of intimacy. Neither relationship led to a permanent recoupling, yet both were extremely positive for her.

EMMA'S STORY

Emma was one of those people, not so rare as we might think in this day and age, who arrive at age forty having had only one sexual partner in her life. As you may recall, Emma's husband was a rigid perfectionist; he always had to run the show and was prone to issuing orders to those around him, especially Emma. After their separation, she still didn't understand why she hadn't enjoyed their sex life more. She imagined it had somehow been her "fault" that she wasn't very "good" in bed—an impression that her ex-husband's criticisms had done nothing to dispel.

The fact was, Emma had had only a fleeting acquaintance with orgasm. She was too inexperienced to realize that her husband's lack of sexual sensitivity and proficiency had as much, or more, to do with her inability to reach orgasm as her own lack of skill.

By the time she'd been separated a few months, Emma was doing plenty of things she enjoyed, either alone or with friends; she soon felt pretty good about her life. She found she didn't need her husband telling her what to do, or how to do it; she was much better off answering to herself instead of him.

But resuming life as a sexual being was still a big issue for Emma. She wondered, "What would I do with someone else? How would it go? How would I feel?"

One evening, Emma received a phone call from Nick, a guy she'd known in high school. They'd dated once or twice back then; nothing serious. She hadn't seen him in over twenty years, until a recent class reunion brought them together. They'd chatted briefly and Emma had mentioned she was on her own again. Nick lived in another city now. Over the phone he said he was coming to town on business in a couple of weeks and wondered if she'd like to get together for dinner.

Emma thought, "Why not?" and agreed to go out with him. During dinner, she received the message, loud and clear, that what really interested Nick was sex. There was nothing overt or

vulgar about it: just a certain intensity in his manner, the prover-
bial gleam in his eye. Emma suspected Nick was still married,
although he was vague and a little self-contradictory on the subject, and she didn't really care enough one way or the other to
press him about it.

As it turned out, Nick passed through town every two or three
months. He promised to call her next time, and was as good as his
word. Reciprocating his hospitality, Emma invited him to dinner at
her place, and they had a pleasant but uneventful evening. On another occasion, they went out to a movie and had a drink afterwards.

By now, Emma had been separated for a year and a half. The
next time Nick called to say he had a business trip coming up,
she thought: "He still wants to go to bed with me, I can tell. Well,
so do I." Her sexual drive had reasserted itself sufficiently to overcome her diffidence and shyness, as well as her anxiety over what
the experience would be like.

After dinner at a nice restaurant, Emma invited Nick back to the
house for coffee and a liqueur. They began making out on the sofa,
and eventually she led him to the bedroom. His eagerness to follow
her didn't surprise Emma in the least. Far more surprising, however,
was her discovery of what a good experience it was. The sex was
quite marvelous, and she had an orgasm, the first she'd had in years.
Not only that, Nick told her with obvious sincerity that she was an
absolute delight in bed, which made her feel just wonderful.

For about a year, Emma saw Nick every couple of months.
They always had a good time making love, even though it was
clear to her that theirs was primarily a sexual relationship and little
more. Eventually, however, she tired of the relationship's limita-
tions and decided to end it. When Nick realized there would be
no more sex, he stopped calling. This was fine with Emma, because in the meantime, she'd become involved with someone else.

His name was Mark, a bright, attractive, extremely interesting
man slightly younger than she, who had behaved considerately
toward her. Emma had met him through a bridge group she'd
joined, four tables of bridge players who met at a different mem-
ber's house every week. She and Mark started dating, and found
a tremendous compatibility between them. Their relationship developed beautifully. Sexually, it was great: They enjoyed each
other. Mark made her feel special.

There was just one problem: Mark had three kids, the youngest of whom was seven years old, who lived with him part-time. Emma's only child was already in his freshman year at college. Did she really want to get too involved with a man who was going to be raising three children for years to come, when she'd finished raising hers?

Although that question hovered at the back of Emma's mind, it didn't stop her from getting all the benefit she could from the relationship, the best she'd ever enjoyed with a man. Then fate intervened to resolve the issue. Mark's company transferred him to Chicago.

Since she had a growing real-estate practice, Emma didn't feel able or willing to move to another city. She and Mark agreed to try to keep the relationship going by commuting on weekends as often as they could, and talking on the phone in between. This arrangement worked for a while, but soon the visits and phone calls became fewer, and Emma gathered that Mark had met somebody else. That hurt a little, but in the end she decided she could accept it. There were just too many practical obstacles to making their relationship permanent. Today, she and Mark consider themselves friends and trade the odd phone call and birthday card—meanwhile, he has married the woman in Chicago.

Even though both of these intimate relationships didn't last, each played an important pat in Emma's life. With Nick, she learned she has a healthy sexual drive and can function perfectly well in bed, contrary to her ex-husband's opinion. The relationship with Mark reinforced that knowledge, but also proved she could be sexually and emotionally intimate with someone in a truly adult way. She recognized that both she and Mark had other strong needs besides their need for each other, and she wasn't willing to sacrifice everything else in her life to save the relationship at all costs.

SEX IN THE ADULT RELATIONSHIP

Emma and her two lovers illustrate how intimacy in an adult relationship differs from intimacy in an adolescent one.

Underlying the adolescent relationship (and remember, we're speaking about relationships we make not only in our teens, but right through our twenties), there is an implicit equation at work, more or less unconsciously. Simply put, it goes something like this: *Dinner = Bed = Love = Marriage.*

The equation is entirely appropriate for people at that stage of life. Psychologically, adolescents and postadolescents are at a stage of their development where one of the major tasks is learning to maintain a one-to-one relationship. So it's appropriate for two adolescents who are strongly attracted to develop an exclusive relationship very quickly: to go steady, to hold hands on the way home from school, to consider it "wrong" to get too friendly with anybody else of the opposite sex. And as young adults become established in their lives, they translate this drive to exclusivity into the equation above.

In so doing, they are aided and abetted by the powerful biological imperative to procreate. There is frequently an implied bargain, not always acted on, but nonetheless there, as a potential basis for commitment: "If I go to bed with you, you have to love me. If you love me, I'll love you, and we'll get married and have kids and . . ."

In an adult relationship—say, from the mid-to-late thirties onward—a different dynamic is at work. You're no longer learning to develop one-to-one relationships. And, depending on your age, you may no longer be driven by the need to procreate. That isn't what sex and intimacy are about anymore. Now sex is something that happens by choice between two consenting adults. While it often involves emotional closeness and genuine caring, in addition to plain old lust, it no longer involves the adolescent equation.

Adults are freer to choose what the sexual experience means to them—and what, if anything, it will lead to. Emma and Nick were two consenting adults who agreed to have sex. Neither had any illusions that the act was intended to lead to a permanent commitment. In the case of Emma and Mark, exclusive commitment was possible for a time, but ran its course when other adult imperatives intervened. Now Emma has reached a point in her life where serial monogamy might well become the norm.

MONOGAMY IF NECESSARY, BUT NOT NECESSARILY MONOGAMY

Another patient of mine, a social worker in her late thirties named Theresa, became heavily involved in several activities that absorbed a great deal of her interest and energy: a women's discussion group, a support organization for divorced Catholics, and a naturalists' club. For the first year after her separation, she wasn't sexually active. Through her various activities, she met and eventually dated several different men, but preferred to keep the relationships platonic.

After dating one of these men over several months, Theresa went out with him to an Italian restaurant on a Friday night. They'd been there before and had a good time; this evening they had an even better time—the relationship was really growing on both of them. Afterward, they returned to his place for dessert—and wound up having a wonderful time making love. They parted the next morning, promising to get together soon.

Theresa went home, showered and changed, and went about her usual Saturday errands. That evening, she had a date with another of the men she'd been seeing. She'd known him, too, for several months. They went to an early movie on Saturday evening, then back to his place for a late supper. Later, one thing led to another and, lo and behold, she went to bed with him, too.

When Theresa came in to see me the following week, she was genuinely amazed at herself for what she'd done on the weekend—and a little perplexed that she didn't feel more guilty. She'd never been "promiscuous" in her life, and yet she had to admit she didn't feel particularly promiscuous now, either. She discovered she could accept the idea that these two relationships had evolved independently of each other, and had simultaneously reached a point where it was appropriate that sex became part of the relationship. Neither was a singles-bar pickup or a one-night stand. In both cases, there was honest affection and trust.

A couple of months later, Theresa stopped dating the second man and began an exclusive, monogamous relationship with the first man. But she was aware that she was playing by different ground rules than the ones adolescents use. In the end, the exclusive relationship lasted eighteen months, then she resumed dating different people. Dinner did not have to mean bed, did not have to mean love, did not have to mean marriage. And having more than one sexual partner didn't have to mean wanton promiscuity, either.

Whether or not you're strictly monogamous, the key elements in any adult sexual relationship are trust and respect between partners. These imply seeing your partner as a person, not an object—and in turn, being seen in that light yourself. That's different from the old adolescent way of relating. When we relate on a "You take care of me, I'll take care of you" level, then we're both objects—whereas in adult sexual encounters, we're both persons with minds of our own, responsible to and for ourselves.

This also means you should get to know the other person at least a little before rushing into bed: It's harder to extend genuine trust and respect to someone you've only just met.

BARRIERS TO INTIMACY

Seeing potential partners as objects instead of as persons raises barriers to authentic intimacy. It's hard to get close to the reality of another person when you're casting them in a role, instead of just letting them be themselves.

Andy was a thirty-five-year-old advertising salesman at a radio station, whose wife had left him and their son and daughter, aged ten and eight. Initially, Andy felt totally overwhelmed, adrift. He hunkered down, toughed out the deep-black-pit period, and realized that he and the kids could survive after all.

In the process, Andy became heavily involved in the routines of work, child care, and housekeeping, to the exclusion of practically everything else. At my suggestion, he eventually joined a single-parents' group, where he found support and encouragement. The group was also a good way to meet some new people. In the course of doing group activities that included the children, he met Monique, a secretary in her early thirties who had a five-year-old daughter. It was actually Monique who suggested they do something together, without their kids.

On a weekend when Andy's ex-wife had the children, he and Monique took all of Saturday to go around the city and have some fun. They started with brunch, did some strolling and window-shopping, took in a movie, and finally, drove out of town to a flea market in the country. After dinner in a pretty little town neither of them had ever visited before, they dashed back to the city so Monique could be home by eight o'clock when her ex-husband dropped off her daughter.

Andy drove home in a daze. He'd had such a good time, he couldn't believe how fast the day had gone. There was something magical about being with Monique. She was high-spirited, eager, full of curiosity about the world. My gosh, he thought: I think I'm falling for her.

For months previously, he'd been anxious about everything, worrying about his own future and being overprotective of his kids, trying hard to be both father and mother to them. In Monique, he saw an answer to all his problems.

Unfortunately, Andy built up the relationship so much in his mind that when he and Monique finally went to bed, he was impotent with her. He had weighed down the event with such vast and all-consuming significance, not only for himself but for his children, that his anxieties interfered with his sexual functioning. This is a common enough experience for men, especially if a relationship is just beginning, and they feel a lot is riding on it. The third time he and Monique went to bed, however, Andy was relaxed enough to maintain an erection throughout, and it was a good experience for both of them.

At that point, he surrendered to the adolescent equation: He was in love. He psyched himself up for a caretaking–caregiving relationship between himself and Monique. He imagined Monique as the new mom for his kids. It lasted all of three more months before Monique broke it off. Andy was expecting too much of her. There was no way she was going to be a mom to his two kids as well as her own child, and a mom to him, too.

But all was not lost, because the relationship accomplished two important things for Andy. He learned that he could function sexually again. And he realized, after rueful reflection (and some discussion with his favorite shrink), that he really didn't need to go searching for a mom for his children. It was inappropriate to cast someone in that role who wasn't seeking it. He and his children didn't need a savior anyway; they were all learning to manage quite well on their own; he could relax a bit about being a single parent. It had been awfully tough at first, but it was amazing how good the kids were becoming at making lunches for themselves, and otherwise taking more responsibility around the house.

Now, many months later, Andy is involved in another relationship with a woman. It's going well, and this time they're keeping their residences separate.

Another barrier to intimacy is fear of being hurt again, which can make a person wary about getting too close to someone. It's a barrier that is more likely to be raised in the months immediately following separation, and less likely to be raised later, provided people have worked through their grieving and let go of their pain. Some people maintain the barrier for an awfully long time.

Melissa, a forty-three-year-old travel agent, had been married twice, both times unhappily. She had a bubbly sense of humor and great social skills, and had successfully made the transition from grieving the breakup to socializing and dating, as described in the last chapter. Her dinner parties were always a hit, and she received plenty of return invitations from friends, married and unmarried. She liked men and sex. But at some level, deep down, Melissa didn't want to get hurt again, and she used the old adolescent equation to keep intimacy at bay, even when intimacy, or at least lovemaking, was the one thing she craved most.

Whenever Melissa dated a man, she unfailingly approached the date as if it were going to lead to marriage. She immediately sized each guy up as potential marriage material, checking out his professional status, his salary, his car, his qualifications to be a father to her two teenagers. And, just as unfailingly, she found something seriously wrong with each man after two or three dates. They didn't fit some magical mold that Melissa had constructed in her mind.

She became interested in one man through having him as a client. From serving his travel needs, she knew he had a senior position with a big corporation, and that he frequently traveled to interesting destinations for both business and pleasure—and there was never a "Mrs." along for the ride.

When he invited Melissa out for dinner, she accepted willingly. They had a fine meal and an enjoyable evening together. Then the judging began. Even though Melissa liked the fellow and found him extremely attractive, and even though he was more than well-heeled enough to treat her in style, she concluded he was far too busy with his work; she'd be better off not to get involved with him after all. Besides, he traveled so much, she wouldn't see him half the time!

But was that any reason not to date him? Was that any reason not to go to bed with him, since sex had become such an important issue for her? The man may not have been ideal marriage material, but he was certainly promising date material.

Melissa was undermining herself by maintaining a fantasy: that Mr. Right was out there somewhere, and he was going to come along and save her and make things perfect. As long as she maintained that fantasy, she wouldn't have to risk intimacy, wouldn't get hurt. But she wouldn't have any fun, either.

The fact was, Melissa needed intimacy, so her behavior was highly self-defeating. Increasingly, she felt bitter about her lot in life. "It never works out for me," she complained.

THE ETIQUETTE OF INTIMACY

When sex reenters the life of the separated person or single parent, it raises certain questions about how to behave—questions of manners and morals, and also practical questions. For one, what about sexually transmitted diseases (STDs)? For another, what about the children—how much should they know about a parent's love life?

In the age of AIDS (Acquired Immune Deficiency Syndrome), there's a great deal to be said for knowing your partner, and especially your partner's state of health. If you're going to be sexually intimate as an adult, you're certainly well within your rights to ask a first-time partner if he or she has been diagnosed with an STD: not only AIDS, but the more commonly transmitted ailments, such as herpes, or chlamydia. Given the high incidence of these diseases, it's not an insult to inquire, merely a sensible precaution.

Of course, it's conceivable that a potential partner could lie to you and conceal the fact that he or she is carrying an STD—or he/she may simply be unaware of the fact. But for your own protection, it's wise to ask—and wiser still to insist on safe sex, that is, using a condom—at least until you're satisfied that the other person is disease-free.

If, on the other hand, you yourself have been diagnosed as having an active STD, it's only ethical to inform your partner. If a case of herpes, say, is in remission, or at a low level of transmissibility, you can feel more confident about having sex. If your case is an active one, you should refrain from sexual intercourse altogether. To risk infecting your partner(s) is hardly showing them respect.

As for allowing your children to know you're sexually active, there are a couple of basic ground rules to follow. The first ground rule was just as true during your marriage as it is now: Your sexual life is private, not something for your kids to know about in any detail. What you do in bed is your business, and that of the consenting adult you're with.

The second ground rule is that you don't hide from your children the fact that you're dating. Sometimes you may feel tempted to do so, because consciously or unconsciously you want to maintain their fantasy that you and their other parent will get back together someday. (Indeed, you may even indulge in the fantasy yourself.) But it's not constructive to hide your dates away from the children's eyes.

Chances are you'll find that your kids, after some initial shyness or suspicion of the person you're dating, will accept the idea that you're resuming a social life. Mom (or Dad) is normal, after all! Your older children may have been worried about you, feeling they had to entertain your or cheer you up in your loneliness. Your dating relieves them of that burden.

Your children don't have to meet every person you date, but if you're seeing someone for the third or fourth time and getting semi-serious about this person, it's a good idea to introduce him or her to your children when it's convenient. Your kids may get anxious about this person if they don't know who he or she is—just as you would worry about who *their* friends are if you knew nothing about them. If such friends are kept a big dark secret, you wonder what the problem is. If your children meet the person you're seeing and discover that he or she is a reasonable human being and not an ogre, they'll feel a lot more comfortable and accepting.

You don't need your kids' approval of the people you date— again, you're responsible *for* your children, not *to* them—but you should introduce them to your dates for the sake of honesty and openness in all your relationships. Also, your children may fear, "You're getting all involved with Jack or Mary, and you're going to forget about *us.*" You may have to reassure them that your involvement with Jack or Mary doesn't exclude your caring about your kids. It will be easier to reassure them if they've already met Jack or Mary, and come to realize they're reasonable people.

Finally, if you want Jack or Mary to sleep over at your place, it will be easier on the children if they meet him or her first. It can be upsetting for children to encounter a total stranger at the breakfast table. You could let them know your guest is staying over and will be there in the morning, to avoid rude surprises.

You don't have to answer to your children about whom you sleep with: Just be sensitive to their reactions. Initially, they may respond to the new person as a threat, but if you handle the situation naturally and matter-of-factly, the children will accept it more easily.

A footnote: Some single parents may ask, "If I have a lover sleeping over, how can I refuse my teenage son or daughter when they demand the same privilege?" The answer is that the ground rules for your adult relationships are different from adolescent relationships—as we've been saying all along. You're still the adult and head of the household: You decide what the houses rules are.

CAROL'S STORY

The last time we saw Carol, she was happily living in her new house and socializing with her community of friends at the tennis club. With these building blocks of her new life firmly in place, mortared by a sense of well-being that came from learning to be un-dependent, it was only a matter of time before Carol entered an intimate relationship that worked for her.

She'd gradually gotten to know Glenn, an investment analyst, through her work on the club's executive board. As treasurer, Glenn had provided Carol with financial information and other valuable assistance during the successful membership drive she'd organized.

At first, they didn't exactly date—just had coffee or a drink together in the club bar after meetings. When Glenn asked Carol out for dinner, it would be their first social engagement outside the confines of the club, and she felt a little uncomfortable about it. If the relationship didn't work out, she wondered, how would it affect their ability to work together on the executive board? Would she feel self-conscious about running into him at the tennis club? This was a genuine concern, since the club had become such a big part of her life.

Nonetheless, she decided to pursue the relationship and see where it would lead. She liked Glenn, as far as she could tell; the only way to learn if she'd like him better was to get to know him better. Although she'd dated a few men since her separation from Richard, and even slept with a couple of them, she'd had no "serious" relationships yet. The men she'd dated had all seemed rather shallow and immature. At forty-six, with both his children by a former marriage now grown, Glenn, who was seven years older than Carol, seemed to know who he was, while content to let others be themselves also.

After dating him a few times, Carol came in to tell me all about Glenn. With a little twinkle in her eye, she admitted that she was beginning to feel very fond of him. He had brains, a self-deprecating wit, and a lovely sense of fun. In fact—she reddened slightly—they were even talking about going away on a trip. Both of them had a lot of accumulated leave at work; why not spend some of it together?

Why not indeed, said I. And off they went on an autumn tour of New England.

Beforehand, they sat down to pore over tourist brochures and plan their itinerary together, picking out some interesting bed-and-breakfast places in New Hampshire and Massachusetts. As a former West Coast girl, Carol was eager to explore the East Coast. And as luck would have it, they hit a week of Indian summer. They drove in mild, hazy October sunshine under trees in their fall colors, past beautiful seascapes, through charming towns of clapboard houses and picket fences. They visited Cape Cod and took the ferry across to Nantucket. They hiked, tried deep-sea fishing, ate and slept well. They experienced real pleasure.

One of the things that struck Carol most, as she described it to me later, was how different the trip had been from her memories of traveling with Richard. She'd always been afraid to suggest anything to Richard, in case it wasn't what he wanted, Richard would get irritated if she were late getting ready, or if he had to stop the car so she could go to the bathroom. With Glenn, there was a different atmosphere entirely: Each would state what they wanted to do; they'd discuss it and work something out. They could give and take suggestions easily, plan together flexibly. And if they had to stop because one of them wanted to admire the view, that was fine too. "It's such a pleasure just to be myself," Carol said. "I feel grown-up now."

She felt the same way later, even after they returned home and

Glenn began spending weekends at Carol's house. It was great having him there, doing things they enjoyed, curling up by the fireplace together on a Friday or Saturday evening. But there was, as well, a spirit of live and let live. One weekend, when Glenn had to visit his father in Montreal and Carol had a bad cold, she felt okay about saying she'd rather stay behind; she'd go and meet Glenn's father another time. In the bad old days, Richard would have been upset and insinuated that she had to accompany him, cold or no cold. Now, with Glenn, there was a mutual understanding: Both of them had their independence and their freedom of choice.

Even so, as she and Glenn grew closer, Carol found she had to be careful not to let him slip into a caretaker role toward her. Like many men of his generation, Glenn had been well-conditioned to play that role—to protect and take care of the female. He wanted to come over and mow her lawn, for instance, but Carol, who had been mowing it for months, declined with thanks and told him she could take care of it herself.

The need to be protective of her own space didn't stop her from sharing and enjoying all sorts of things with Glenn. At the club, they discovered that not only could they continue working well on the executive board, but they could play well together too. They started entering doubles tournaments, and although they didn't win any trophies, they had a good time.

As Carol put it to me: "Basically, Glenn wants the same kind of relationship I do. It has to be give and take. But there are some things I will not take, and some I will not give."

BILL'S STORY

The next time I saw Bill, he'd survived The Big Date with Charlene—and had gone out with her three more times. Four dates already! They were really moving along.

The first date, at Charlene's company's banquet, had gone surprisingly well. Bill had actually enjoyed talking with all those computer types. Even more important, Charlene had been fun to be with—they'd really hit it off. And, of course, his sexual anxieties had been irrelevant, because they didn't go anywhere near a bed.

The second time they dated, it was just the two of them, and they went to dinner at a favorite restaurant of Charlene's. The more Bill got to know her, the more interesting he found her. "You know," he told me, "this gal goes scuba diving! She impresses the hell out of me. She's had vacations down in Florida and even takes her kid with her."

The "kid" was a fifteen-year-old son who divided his time between weekdays at his mother's place and weekends at his father's, and who seemed reasonably well-adjusted (for a fifteen-year-old). Bill was fascinated by the way Charlene and her ex-husband handled their continuing relationship, which revolved solely around their son, in such a constructive, cooperative manner.

This was the first time Bill had made friends with another single parent. It was a novel and intriguing experience for him to share parenting problems and to get helpful ideas and advice for dealing with them.

Recently, Charlene had gone on a diving vacation by herself, leaving her son with his father. "Her ex sounds like a pretty decent guy," Bill commented. "Funny, I'm starting to get the picture of what it's like for an ex-wife. It sort of helps me to see Marie's side of things."

For instance, Charlene's ex-husband had a higher-paying job than hers, so he made monthly support payments to help her out with the mortgage. But once or twice the check had been late, disrupting Charlene's financial arrangements; and it reminded Bill of the times he'd been behind with his own payments to Marie and the children. "I figure she's got a right to know when the money's coming in. That was their deal. She's got bills to pay and plans to make."

Similarly, Bill learned from Charlene how dearly she valued her weekends, when she had some time for herself. "I guess that must be true for Marie too. I can see why Marie seems so happy when Lisa and Jordan come to stay with me. She's not really dumping them on me."

In the middle of all this, Bill and Charlene had started sleeping together. Judging by the happy grin on his face, that side of things was going well too.

At a later session, Bill talked about the difference between his sex life with Charlene and his previous experiences. It was something of a revelation to him that lovemaking could mean so much more than the routine physical act it had become with Marie. Bill saw that he and Marie had treated each other like objects, physically as well as psychologically. Now, having sex had become an exploratory act, an extension of the emotional intimacy he and Charlene were creating between them.

"It's real different," he admitted, "having sex with a person, and feeling like one yourself. . . . It's not just something you do to get off, if you know what I mean."

Bill found he was drinking less now. He was so involved in his new relationships with Charlene and his male friends, so absorbed in his various activities outside of work, that he didn't think of alcohol as the answer to every problem.

Bill's relationship with Charlene also had a little to do with the fact that she was his own age, and he couldn't "father" her, as he had Marie. Charlene was worldly and experienced, and Bill learned things from her—not in a didactic, teacher-student fashion, but simply by observing her in action. He'd never had such close-up experience of a truly adult woman.

"You know, she's practically like one of the guys," he marveled. "She has a job, she travels, she takes responsibility for raising her kid. And when she says 'No,' she really means 'No.'"

From the shine of appreciation in his eyes, I could see Bill was finding an adult relationship far more rewarding than a adolescent caretaker-caretakee relationship.

Chapter Ten

To Recouple or Not?

A s I mentioned at the beginning of the book, I never advise patients to divorce—but then, I never advise them to marry, either. People will do the darndest things anyhow, regardless of what I might tell them. Similarly, I never advise whether or not to recouple—but that doesn't mean I don't give general advice on the subject.

You'd certainly expect that folks would think twice before re-coupling after separation or divorce. It's a big, life-shaping deci-sion to cohabit with someone—to make another exclusive, monogamous commitment—especially after emerging from the ruins of a previous relationship. At the very least, you'd expect people to stop and ask themselves, "Am I ready to do this? To take the risks and make the compromises this new commitment re-quires? How likely am I to repeat the errors of the past? If it doesn't work out, am I prepared to handle another painful separation?"

Surprisingly often, men and women rush into recoupling soon after a former relationship has ended—sometimes immediately af-terward—going straight from one commitment to the other with-out a breathing space in between. In Chapter 3, we called this the rebound relationship. I've seen many people recouple far too quickly, without digesting the meaning of the previous separation, or without learning about their own needs and how to meet them better. They persuade themselves they've found a better caretaker, only to discover cracks in the new relationship beginning to appear within a year or two—the same cracks as in the last one, only showing up more quickly.

With so many people acting in this way, it's easy to see why research shows that second marriages are no happier, and have even less likelihood of succeeding, than first marriages.

But it doesn't have to be that way—especially if you've read this book! By now, you know that finding someone new to take care of, or to take care of you (all in the name of love), isn't any magic route to happiness.

I'm not trying to discourage you from recoupling after a separa-tion. Instead, I'm encouraging you to learn how to meet your own adult needs first—and I'm saying a spouse or partner is irrelevant to that process. Once you've learned more about your needs and how to fulfill them, your prospects for recoupling happily will be greatly enhanced.

This final chapter, then, deals with the issues involved in decid-ing whether to recommit yourself to being part of a monogamous couple. That's entirely different from making a decision to date someone, or even to have sex with them. It entails fundamental choices about how you're going to live the rest of your life—and how you can continue being yourself within any relationship, per-manent or temporary.

THE LONG AND WINDING ROAD

When patients are passing through the long dark night that falls immediately after separation, I often tell them: "You're hurting badly now, wishing you had a love relationship that would last forever. Well, you're not going to believe this—but in a year or two, you won't see a relationship as the only answer. You may even wonder if you're really ready for the compromises needed to make a relationship work. Who knows, you may decide to stay on your own a while."

At that point, patients probably doubt my sanity. They're feeling as if their world has ended and they'll never feel joy or happiness again, unless they can miraculously find Mr. or Ms. Right to save them: any port in a storm, as the saying goes. If anybody offered them another chance at love, they'd jump at it.

I imagine you've felt like that, too. But here you are, say, a year, two, or even three after your separation, and the world looks like a very different place. You can see that there *was* light at the end of the tunnel, and it wasn't a train after all.

By now, you've made some really significant gains in finding out about yourself. You've practiced becoming responsible to and for yourself. You've learned how to be selfish, but in a constructive and ethical way. You've discovered how to play and have fun—not only in games, but in relationships. You've truly put your dead marriage or relationship behind you, even though you still think about it sometimes.

It seems like ages since that long, dark night. Maybe you're now involved with someone you care about—maybe you're not, but would like to be. And you wonder, "Do I actually want to recouple again—in a serious, long-term, committed way? Do I want to live together? Do I want to make it *permanent?*"

The answers to these questions aren't as simple as they used to be. You no longer view your happiness as depending on a love relationship, no matter what the cost. You have other needs that have to be given their due, weighed in the balance against the advantages and disadvantages of recoupling.

CONSTRUCTIVE COMPROMISES

If you've successfully established yourself on your own again, having learned to live in an un-dependent way, you'll recognize there are compromises to make in sharing your life with someone else. These compromises are real. They're also necessary, no matter how much you love the other person, if the relationship is going to work.

Such compromises don't have to be insurmountable obstacles to recoupling. Just remember they *are* compromises, involving a reasonable degree of give and take on both sides, not concessions: not sacrifices of your individuality, or needs, as a person. Compromises have to be constructive for both of you.

Think of these compromises as parallel to sharing your living space with a roommate. There, you have to make compromises too, or the arrangement doesn't work. You have to leave your roommate half the shelf space in the refrigerator. You have to take shorter showers so you don't use up all the hot water and leave none for the other person. These are the constructive, practical sorts of compromises you have to be prepared to make in sharing your physical environment.

In a much deeper sense, sharing your emotional and psychological space also requires making some accommodations for your partner. It entails a willingness to be intimate, to be emotionally available to the other person. It entails giving up some of the control you've had over your existence.

But that doesn't mean what it used to mean in your former adolescent relationships. Then, you stopped being yourself, in order to be a good little boy or girl. You stopped being yourself in order to be a good provider or caretaker.

Now, you don't stop being yourself in exchange for having a relationship: That's no longer the bargain. You can rightfully expect to be who you are, and to be cared about as a person. And at the same time, you're prepared to treat your partner in the same way. If you're ready to do that, then you're ready to recouple, with a pretty good shot at happiness. If you're not prepared to do that, you shouldn't recouple—unless, of course, you want to duplicate the old adolescent relationship, for which you'll still have to answer to yourself for the consequences.

The basic idea in recoupling is creating an *equal partnership*. That's what adults do. There's no leader and no follower, the way there was in the adolescent, caretaker-caretakee relationship. Just as in a business partnership, you make accommodations for your partner, treating him or her fairly and equally, as you yourself want to be treated.

A love relationship may not be a business deal, but they have some features in common. For instance, when our friend Bill eventually brought Mario, his manager, into the carpet business as a partner, Bill had to let go of some of his control over management of the business. Mario didn't want to be a partner in name only. But in return, Bill gained personal freedom. Because he had a partner, some of his time and energy were freed up so he could devote them to other important interests, such as his friendships, his lover Charlene, his kids, and his golf game.

Similarly, committing yourself to a new exclusive relationship requires giving up some of the control you used to exercise over your daily existence when you were single. But it can also free you and benefit you in a great variety of ways—emotionally, physically, socially—even intellectually and spiritually. If it doesn't, you have to ask what the relationship is really worth to you, and whether it's worth compromising for. Would the benefits of recoupling be great enough to make the compromises worthwhile? That's the question everyone has to answer to his or her own satisfaction.

ANSWERING THE QUESTION

Different folks will inevitably come up with different answers to that question. For some, the answer will clearly be: "No, I'm not ready yet. Maybe later, or with someone else, but not right now." For others, the answer will be clear: "Yes, I've learned to respect and trust and love this person. We both feel committed to spending our lives together. And this time, I'm going to do it right." And for yet other folks, the situation may remain indefinite: "I'm not sure yet. I value this relationship, but I don't want to rush blindly into a commitment. I'll wait a while and see how life unfolds."

In the last chapter, we saw how Emma, the real estate woman, resolved the question in the first way. She wasn't prepared to sacrifice the career she'd built in order to move to Chicago with her boyfriend, Mark.

An example of the second resolution was Larry, the department store van driver from Chapter 8, and his girlfriend, Jill, who lived in the same apartment building and looked after his kids. They committed to living together and eventually married—but only after satisfying themselves that they had a solid base of shared interests, personal compatibility, trust, and respect.

The middle ground between these positions was occupied by my patient Phil. A forty-something administrator at city hall, Phil had been quite devastated by the breakup of his childless marriage, but managed to tough out the first year on his own without rushing into a rebound relationship. In the second year, he became intimate with Jean, a delightful woman who had two daughters, twelve and ten.

Phil had always wanted children. Although he didn't move in with Jean, he stayed at her place on weekends and started getting involved in her children's lives—treating them to a movie, driving them to their lessons, and other activities. He thought it would be wonderful to "play Dad." But in reality, it was a lot tougher than he'd expected. The older daughter began having difficulties with her mom and decided to move in with her father. Relations in Phil's "adopted" family became very strained, and he discovered what a thankless task being a stepparent can sometimes be: "You're not my *real* dad!"

It was unfortunate that Phil's well-meaning efforts weren't better rewarded, because his relationship with Jean was a good one. They enjoyed spending time together, especially traveling to nearby cities to take in plays and visit art galleries and museums. But in time, Phil discovered there were too many differences between himself and Jean—personality, life-style, and cultural traits that just didn't "fit," as he put it. Jean felt this, too, so in the end they decided not to make their relationship permanent.

With his friend Sharon, on the other hand, Phil quickly found a meeting of minds. Sharon was a lawyer who had never married and had no intention of doing so. But she and Phil developed a close relationship, based on getting together once or twice a month. He'd spend the weekend at her apartment, and they'd go around the city together, having a great time doing things they both liked. At the root of their closeness was a strong commonality of interests and experiences: Sharon and Phil shared a common cultural and religious background, which equipped them with a whole range of nonverbal understandings. They felt they'd been "hatched in the same place," Phil told me, and this instinctive knowledge made their relationship so much easier and more natural.

Phil found this relationship met his need for intimacy with a woman. Like Sharon, he was quite content with its part-time nature, and he felt no compulsion to recouple on a permanent, full-time basis.

Incidentally, I'm not suggesting that you try to seek out someone "just like yourself," since such a person doesn't exist. But, on balance, it tends to be true that the chances for a successful relationship are greater if the two of you share enough cultural background that the connection feels right—that it makes a kind of psychological sense. At the very least, in cross-cultural marriages, the lack of common cultural background needs to be compensated for by a willing openness to, and honest respect for, the differences in your partner's upbringing, experiences, and values.

JOYCE'S SOLUTION

There are alternative ways of resolving the question of recoupling. It doesn't even necessarily have to include a romantic relationship—a fact belatedly discovered by my patient Joyce, a fifty-three-year-old high-school teacher.

Divorced for seven years, Joyce had a lot going for her. She'd done many things right: She loved to dance, so she'd joined a dance group where she made lots of friends; she loved badminton, so she played as often as she could at the racquet club and coached the school team; she was involved in volunteer community work; she was taking courses at night to complete her principal's training. There was just one thing Joyce wasn't doing right: She had a lot of difficulty being responsible to and for herself. She still thought she needed a caretaker.

In the seven years since her divorce, Joyce had been through three relationships with men, two of them alcoholics. Her ex-husband had also been an alcoholic. As each relationship started, Joyce immediately fell into the caregiver role. And of course, alcoholics just love being taken care of, to the point where they often abuse their caregiver as much as they abuse alcohol. Joyce was a marvelous caregiver, a consummate mother (her two children were now grown up), a wonderfully warm, generous, understanding person, and she expected to be treated in kind. But that approach just didn't work in her *adult* relationships. She hadn't received much in return from those men, and so was no longer involved with any of them: They hadn't taken care of her.

Joyce's biggest complaint was that she felt lonely. When I told her, "What you really need is to be cared about as a person," she shot back: "What I really need is not to be alone tonight."

One evening, Joyce was chatting with another female teacher during a break in their lecture. Robin, who was in her early thirties, mentioned that her marriage had just broken up, and she needed to place to live fast, to get away from a husband who was becoming abusive. Joyce suggested Robin come to live with her; Joyce's two kids had moved out, leaving a couple of empty rooms, and she could use the extra income. Robin was delighted, and said she'd be willing to pay three hundred dollars a month in rent—and could she move in tomorrow?

Soon Joyce found she was feeling much better. She no longer felt lonely in the evenings; it was awfully nice having someone else in the house when she came home after work. At first, she thought, "Ah, someone new to take care of—someone just separated who's feeling scared and lonely." But she quickly realized that Robin was extremely un-dependent, and didn't want to be looked after—she could look after herself, thank you very much.

They developed a relationship of equals, a kind of partnership. Both had very busy schedules and could manage a sit-down dinner together only two or three times a week—but on those occasions, it was a real pleasure to share the shopping, meal preparation, and washing up, and especially to have the chance to share experiences and talk over the events of the day. They got along like two adults.

Robin lived with Joyce for six months before moving into a place of her own. By that time, Joyce had discovered she could share her own physical and emotional space without having to take care of someone. And she'd discovered she didn't need to sleep with a man in order to feel all right about herself.

"At last," Joyce told me, "I think I know what you've been talking about." Sure, she didn't like being lonely, and sure, she didn't like living alone. But now she knew she could meet her need for companionship without having a man to take care of, or to take care of her. She had options.

In her previous relationships with men, Joyce had abdicated her responsibility for herself; she assumed she had to, in order not to feel lonely. Now she saw there were alternatives between the two poles of abject loneliness and being in a caretaker-caretakee relationship. Today, Joyce still hasn't recoupled, but now she doesn't feel so bad about it. She's enjoying her life, which is really quite rich in activities, achievements, and friendships. For her, that's a breakthrough.

BLENDED FAMILIES

Needless to say, recoupling becomes more complicated with children involved. It's tricky enough when only one partner has kids, and the other has to learn the ropes of becoming a stepparent—without the experience of ever having been a parent. But if both partners have children, the dynamics of the situation grow even more fraught with complications. The more individuals there are in a blended family, the more problematic it can be to make the family function happily.

This is another subject that deserves a whole book to itself. For our purposes, suffice to say it's up to you, the adult, and not your children, to decide whether you want to recouple. And if you do recouple, the process of blending families will be much more successful if you can keep open the lines of communication with your kids. Encourage them to talk about their feelings, worries, fears, and hopes about the whole thing, and be sensitive and responsive to their concerns. Don't imagine they won't have some.

Let's look once again at Larry and Jill, whom we met in Chapter 8. Their marriage brought his son together with her two children, and the new blended family worked out very well. In this,

Larry and Jill definitely had some good fortune. Jill had babysat for Larry before their personal relationship began, so Larry's son Brent had come to know her and her children well; the two adults were actually able to see that their kids got along fine before they all moved in together.

Also, both Larry and Jill were deeply interested in their children's upbringing and education; it felt natural to them to make the family a major focus of their lives, and they devoted a lot of care and energy to making it work. They were willing to invest the effort required. And sometimes that effort is considerable when you have not only your own kids to worry about (and get aggravated by), but your partner's as well.

From the children's point of view, they naturally wonder how your choice of a new partner is going to affect them. Their apprehensions usually reflect a mixture of the emotional and the practical. "Will I like living with him (her)? Will I still see my 'real' Mom (Dad)? Will I have to move? Will his (her) kids move in with us? Do I have to like them?"

Kids feel anxious because they don't know where all these new relationships are going to lead, so it's extremely helpful if they can voice their anxieties and get them out into the open, and receive a sympathetic hearing from you—if, in other words, their feelings can be taken seriously.

Kids get especially upset if a custodial parent's recoupling results in a move to another city, since that inevitably means they'll be seeing less of the noncustodial parent. Most separation or divorce agreements contain a clause that says children can't be moved out of the state or province by one parent without the consent of the other parent. That's fine—but children still need the reassurance of knowing the noncustodial parent will remain a regular presence in their lives. They'll ask, "How will I see my Dad?" And they deserve a clear and honest answer.

I knew one blended family that faced this painful problem and handled it about as well as could be expected. Meredith had sole custody of her three children; Rob had shared custody of his seven-year-old daughter, Julie, who was the same age as Meredith's middle child. They all moved in together, and the arrangement worked reasonably well. Despite the usual rivalries and personality conflicts among the kids, the two families made a pretty good fit.

But the arrangement was threatened when Rob's ex-wife married a Navy officer who was transferred to a base on the East Coast, and Rob's ex-wife wanted to take Julie with her.

This presented a terrible conflict for Rob. He agreed that it was more appropriate for Julie to live primarily with her mom than with him, but he was going to miss Julie terribly. What's more, he felt bad that he'd be stepparenting Meredith's three kids every day, while seeing his own daughter only rarely. What would Julie think? Would she be upset that she was "losing" her dad to another family? Rob was filled with guilt over this. He also experienced great anxiety over the prospect of "losing" Julie.

Rob talked the problem over with his ex-wife, and they worked out a solution. They agreed that Julie needed as much time as possible with her dad to balance the long stretches of absence. Therefore Julie would spend summer vacation, Christmas, and spring break with him, in order to maintain maximum contact without interfering with her education. This agreement allowed Rob to face the separation from his daughter with more confidence and equanimity. Fortunately, the East Coast posting was only for three years, after which there was a good chance Julie and her new family would move back to Rob's city.

STEPPARENTS

In dealing with this development, Rob had to confront another big issue that often results from blending families: accepting the presence of a stepparent in his child's life. Julie's new stepfather would actually be seeing more of her than Rob would; Rob had to extend a great deal of trust to that man, who was going to have quite an influence on Julie's upbringing. Fortunately, Rob met and liked him, and so was able to reassure himself that his daughter wouldn't be harmed by her mother's new relationship.

If you can, try to meet your ex's new partner and get to know him or her a little. It's human nature to perceive that person as a threat. This is especially true if your kids are younger, and you feel you're handing them over to be raised by a stranger. You have to try to see that stranger as a real person and not a thief of your children's affection. You can remind yourself that you've handed your kids over to the care of others before—to babysitters, day-care workers, teachers—and it hasn't harmed your relationship with them.

Now, while a stepparent is admittedly different from a babysitter, a child's attachment to a stepparent is seldom as strong and binding as it is to a natural parent. It helps to remember that no stepparent can "take your place." You and you alone are your child's natural dad or mom, and always will be. Your child knows that with unerring certainty.

At the same time, it's in your children's best interests to develop a good relationship with their stepparent. As the natural parent, you can have an important influence on helping that to happen. If you let your children know it's fine with you if they like their stepparent, it contributes to the making of a positive relationship in a crucial area of their lives.

Finally, if *you* become the new stepparent in the family, you need to face a fundamental fact: Stepparents get a bum rap. You may as well recognize that in your stepchildren's eyes, you're a witch (or monster). The only choice you have in the matter is whether to be an evil witch or a good witch.

Accept the fact that you can never be your stepchildren's "real" parent. It's a mistake to walk into the household and expect them to regard you as they would their natural mom or dad. You'll always be, on some primitive level, an "outsider." That's okay. It doesn't mean you can't develop a very positive relationship with your new partner's kids—as long as you remember you'll always be a stepparent. Just do your best to be a good witch (or monster)—a helpful and influential adult in their lives—instead of an object of fear and loathing.

CAROL'S STORY: CONCLUSION

In the last chapter, we learned about the progress of Carol's intimate relationship with her new friend, Glenn. Since Glenn's two children were grown and living on their own, Carol didn't have to deal with the prospect of mothering them. She and they were able to relate pretty much as adults. But it was still important to her to have friendly relations with them, because, as time went on, she and Glenn became quite serious about each other. Finally, when it felt as if their relationship had achieved a kind of critical mass, they decided to try living together in Carol's house.

Nonetheless, once bitten, twice shy: Both of them had a few doubts about risking their independence for the sake of living together. Glenn thought it might be wise to keep his apartment for a while just in case. He knew how things could go wrong in a relationship, and felt more comfortable knowing he had an escape hatch. Carol agreed; she didn't feel threatened by the idea. Both of them knew that, no matter how much they loved each other, they'd have to learn to make compromises in living together, and it might ease the process if Glenn didn't need to panic about the immediate loss of his own living space.

Carol also recognized that he'd need some space of his own in her house. She had an empty second bedroom, which she offered to him as a study, and Glenn gladly accepted. He furnished it with his desk, chair, bookshelves, and personal computer. They also agreed that he should move his dining-room suite into the house, since it complemented Carol's decor beautifully. This seemed like a good omen. Both of them had high hopes for living together, but at this stage, they were still just trying out the arrangement. By taking a wait-and-see attitude, neither felt trapped.

After several months of cohabiting, Carol and Glenn found the relationship *was* indeed working well for them. She was delighted to realize she didn't have to surrender the personal gains she'd made in the past two years, and could carry on with being responsible to and for herself. At the same time, the longer she and Glenn lived together, the better their relationship became: more honest and authentic. They were both able to share a great deal, without giving up their autonomy. Glenn, too, felt reassured. After discussion with Carol, he decided it was okay to give up his apartment.

Shortly after this, Carol told me it was time to terminate her therapy. She was satisfied that she now cared unshakably about herself as a person; and in Glenn, she'd found someone else who cared about her that way, as she did about him.

Appropriately, it was springtime—almost exactly three years since that Easter weekend when Carol's ex-husband Richard had told her he was leaving.

At our last session together, Carol said: "I can see now I tried to get fathered by Richard, and that put a huge burden on our relationship. But now I feel good about myself. It's a feeling that spills over into my work and friendships. My friends all say I look so much happier. I feel empowered." Carol looked directly at me: "I've never been so healthy. I've used up a lot of Kleenex, but it's been worth it."

A few months later, in midsummer, Carol and Glenn were married. I received an announcement in the mail. The following Christmas, I got a lovely card from Carol, telling me how happy she was in her marriage. She added a postscript, which she'd underlined: "And I'm still working at being a person."

BILL'S STORY: CONCLUSION

A year or so after he and Charlene started dating, Bill was feeling comfortably settled in his life as a single person. First of all, his golf game had improved tremendously. He could also go for days without drinking, and usually he drank moderately on social occasions. The carpet business was doing extremely well. Bringing Mario in as a partner had been a great idea, because Mario was a hard and conscientious worker, determined to build up his stake in the company. That was fine with Bill. Now he could give himself permission to take a little time off. He started traveling more and took his two children with him. He was doing more things *with* his kids, instead of *for* them.

Bill and Charlene had enjoyed a lot of good times together. On several occasions, they'd even tried going to baseball games or dinners out with all three of their children. That experiment hadn't worked out so well. Now sixteen, Charlene's son was just a little too old to take an interest in doing things with Lisa or Jordan, so Bill and Charlene didn't force the issue.

They'd talked at times about moving in together, but gradually came to the conclusion it wasn't the right thing for either of them. Bill was sorely tempted by the idea of setting up house with Charlene; he remembered how much he'd once liked certain advantages of married life. Even so, he decided both he and she needed more time for themselves than living together would allow—spaces of their own, where they could do things separately, while still getting together when they wanted to.

"It's a funny thing," Bill admitted to me with a smile, "but a couple of years ago I hated the idea of living alone. Now, I want to spend more time getting to know myself."

Living with someone, he saw, would have interfered with that all-important process right then. For Bill, learning to be a person was still a key issue. This was understandable; he'd been such a role-player most of his life that for years he'd put off getting to know himself.

"This doesn't mean I won't be ready to remarry or live together some day," Bill said. "With Charlene or somebody else. But who knows, maybe I never will. All I know is, for now, I'm not interested in making the compromises."

When he realized he wasn't prepared to commit his whole life to Charlene, Bill felt a pressure lift from him. He'd reached a point where he neither had to recouple at all costs, nor avoid relationships with women. He had other options.

So what was he going to do with his life? He was going to cash in a few of his hard-earned chips and relax and have some fun. He'd made some money selling a piece of the business to Mario, enabling Bill to pay off some debts and reduce his cost of living. Now he thought he'd take a leisurely trip down to the Gulf Coast of Florida and look around for a nice little condominium to invest in—a place where he could spend a few weeks every winter, renting it for the rest of the year through a real estate agent. He wasn't in a rush: He'd just enjoy the process of driving around in the sunshine and scouting the territory, playing a little golf, visiting a cousin who'd moved down there. Life was to be savored now.

And Charlene? Bill remained extremely fond of her. "She's such a great person, Doc, and we've had such great times, I sure want to keep seeing her. We're going to stay close friends, even though we're both free to date other people."

Bill was a little astonished at himself for being able to agree to this last arrangement. Previously, he'd had very proprietary feelings toward his wife, Marie. Since he saw Charlene as a person, however, and not an object, he could understand why she'd want to be free to see other men. He could keep any jealous feelings under control.

"You know, I thought I'd feel a lot more jealous. But it only seems fair, if I've got that freedom, that she should have it too."

Yes, Bill had changed a lot.

POSTSCRIPT

This is where we leave Carol and Bill. And where I must take leave of you, dear reader.

I hope your experience of learning to live on your own again will include some of the successes Carol and Bill enjoyed. Such successes aren't achieved overnight, but when they do come, you'll know you've earned them. And these gains will stay with you: They don't represent an ending, but rather milestones on your continuing journey toward personal growth and fulfillment.

After all the gains you've made in months and perhaps years of effort, you'll know if recoupling is really for you. But whether or not you recouple, you'll still be able to meet your own adult needs: to be responsible to and for yourself; to be cared about for the person you are. While respecting the feelings of others, you'll be able to trust your own.

These are the qualities that make adult life and adult relationships worthwhile. And they are, in fact, the very same qualities that help you live successfully and happily—on your own again.